# The Prodigal Republican

## *Faith and Politics*

## Marc T. Little

WestBow
PRESS

A DIVISION OF THOMAS NELSON

WestBow Press books may be ordered through booksellers or by contacting:

Cover Photo by Bella Vita Photography
Cover Art: Emancipation Proclamation

WestBow Press
A Division of Thomas Nelson
1663 Liberty Drive
Bloomington, IN 47403
www.westbowpress.com
1-(866) 928-1240

ISBN: 978-1-4497-6351-0 (sc)
ISBN: 978-1-4497-6350-3 (hc)
ISBN: 978-1-4497-6827-0 (e)

Library of Congress Control Number: 2012917590

Printed in the United States of America

WestBow Press rev. date: 10/11/2012

# Contents

To my unborn children and the next generation.

# Foreword

Behind every successful person is a cadre of family and friends responsible for helping him achieve his dreams.

I was a Pro Bowl running back with the Denver Broncos and retired as the seventh-leading rusher in NFL history. In 2010, I was immortalized with my induction into the Pro Football Hall of Fame. But to get there I needed love, support, and inspiration from those closest to me. I got all of that and more from my tight-knit family and especially my son, Marc Little.

Marc is not like a regular son. He's also my lawyer, my adviser, and my best friend. Life would be very different if Marc weren't around.

In 1987, while attending the University of Southern California, Marc was robbed at gunpoint. The assailant shot him in the leg. Bleeding to death, Marc was rushed to the hospital and flat-lined several times. His leg had to be amputated, but somehow by the grace of God, he pulled through. When I learned he was going to be okay, I leaned into him and whispered, "If you don't make it, can I have your TV?" His eyes widened and I felt him clutch my arm. "You don't want my TV," he muttered. "Why?" I asked. Sounding as serious as a sermon, Marc said, "Because it's black and white." We burst into laughter as I gave him a hug. We have that kind of joking but loving relationship.

A few years after he recovered, I took Marc to my alma mater, Syracuse University. We were having lunch at The Varsity, a great eatery on the Syracuse campus. The Varsity has been a landmark since my college days, and I took Marc there to soak in the atmosphere and let him experience a slice of my college life. We weren't there five minutes before two students approached our table.

One of them said, "Mr. Little, my friend and I have a bet that we want you to settle. We were discussing what year you were inducted into the Pro Football Hall of Fame. I say it was 1982. My friend says 1984. Who's right?"

I swallowed my drink and looked up at their hopeful faces. "Sorry," I said, "but I've never even been nominated." My voice trailed off. Marc saw the sadness in my eyes that day as I had to tell yet another fan that I wasn't in the Hall of Fame. When we got home, Marc sat down and wrote a letter to the sports editor of the Denver Post detailing why I should be a Hall of Famer. I was blown away by the passion of his letter. So I made a promise to Marc that if I ever did make it to Canton, he would be my presenter.

Twenty years after my promise, Marc was there to present me before a stadium filled with thousands of people and to millions on TV. Marc's words resonated with me and my whole family. He did a magnificent job. He told everyone that either of his two sisters, Christy or Kyra, could have done an excellent job in presenting me, but he was asked to represent our family. I thought that was marvelous.

You can probably tell how much Marc means to me. We are very close. Because he came so close to dying all those years ago, he and I go on a father-son trip somewhere fantastic each year on his birthday to celebrate his life. His passion and zest for life are truly contagious.

A song that we play a lot on those trips is "Wind Beneath My Wings"—not the Bette Midler version, but the Eddie and Gerald Levert version. It's a beautiful rendition with an incredible sax performance. Eddie and Gerald were an incredible father-son musical group. Eddie was the lead singer of the O'Jays back in the 1970s. Gerald performed in some great groups before teaming up with his father. They had many hits including "Wind Beneath My Wings." The song always meant so much to us. But it meant even more after Gerald tragically passed away in 2006 at forty. He was Marc's age.

I have always told Marc that he and his sisters are the wind beneath my wings. As I was watching Marc present me at the Hall of Fame, I was thinking about our incredible relationship. He was telling everyone how much I deserved the honor and how much I meant to him and our family. Then, right at the end of his presentation, he said, "Dad, you are the wind beneath *our* wings!" When I heard that, I lost it. I got up with tears in my eyes. I hugged Marc and said, "You dirty dog. You rolled me under the bus." Marc just looked at me with his eyes flushed and said, "Straighten your tie, Dad. Go knock 'em dead."

Right then, I knew God had saved Marc for me just for that moment.

As you experience the passion and emotion of Marc's book, remember how valuable life is. It is God's favor that you are alive and have air in your lungs and the grace to make every day count.

I greet every morning that way because I am grateful that I have been blessed with Marc. He's my hero. When I finally grow up, I want to be just like him.

—Floyd Little

# Acknowledgements

A special thank you to my bride and best friend, Tegra, who pushed me and encouraged the three-year process of birthing this book. Thank you for listening, for reading, and for showing unwavering patience.

I thank my family for providing a model of conservatism before I knew what *conservative* meant. Specifically, I thank my great aunt, Sinita Walker-Stanley, and her late husband, Rennie Stanley, who were the "original Republicans," and my father, Floyd Little, who gave me a context to understand fiscal conservatism.

I would also like to thank those who inspired me to be openly conservative despite the unpopularity of that stand. Specifically, I thank Supreme Court Justice Clarence Thomas for continuing to stand for conservatism in the face of evil, destructive forces; former Secretary of State Condoleezza Rice for an exemplary life of service and commitment to conservatism and to our nation; economist Thomas Sowell for being a standard-bearer for conservative thought; and the late District Court Judge Robert M. Takasugi for allowing me to be a judicial extern and tenderly helping me discover my conservatism although he was proudly liberal.

I would like to acknowledge those writers who created a body of work that significantly shaped my thoughts: David Barton, Larry Elder, Michael K. Fauntroy, Mark R. Levin, John McWhorter, Shelby Steele, Lee H. Walker, Juan Williams, and Michael Zak.

I also thank Christopher Thomas, Steven "Stevo" Johnson, and Vincent Green whose cravings for black political knowledge, debate, and my conservative perspective during the 2008 election were the impetus for this book.

Finally, I thank my mother, Antoinette, without whom I would not have valued education, would not have appreciated the value of hard work, and would not have discovered Jesus Christ at such an early age. She laid the foundation for me to be the man I am today.

We make a living by what we get, but
we make a life by what we give.

—Unknown

# Introduction:
# The Prodigal Son

The title of this book and the philosophy behind it are based in large measure on the story of the prodigal son found in Luke 15:11–32 (New International Version). While the parable has everything to do with how God handles our sin and our sinful nature, the story also has a practical application to our everyday lives and especially to blacks in America today. I will share a shortened version of the story.

Jesus continued: "There was a man who had two sons. The younger one said to his father, 'Father, give me my share of the estate.' So he divided his property between them.

"Not long after that, the younger son got together all he had, set off for a distant country and there squandered his wealth in wild living. After he had spent everything, there was a severe famine in that whole country, and he began to be in need. So he went and hired himself out to a citizen of that country, who sent him to his fields to feed pigs. He longed to fill his stomach with the pods that the pigs were eating, but no one gave him anything.

"When he came to his senses, he said, 'How many of my father's hired men have food to spare, and here I am starving to death! I will set out and go back to my father and say to him: Father, I have sinned against heaven and against you. I am no longer worthy to be called your son; make me like one of your hired men.'

"So he got up and went to his father. But while he was still a long way off, his father saw him and was filled with compassion for him; he ran to his son, threw his arms around him and kissed him.

"The son said to him, 'Father, I have sinned against heaven and against you. I am no longer worthy to be called your son.'

"But the father said to his servants, 'Quick! Bring the best robe and put it on him. Put a ring on his finger and sandals on his feet. Bring the fattened calf and kill it. Let's have a feast and celebrate. For this son of mine was dead and is alive again; he was lost and is found.' So they began to celebrate.

"Meanwhile, the older son was in the field. When he came near the house, he heard music and dancing. So he called one of the servants and asked him what was going on. 'Your brother has come,' he replied, 'and your father has killed the fattened calf because he has him back safe and sound.'

"The older brother became angry and refused to go in. So his father went out and pleaded with him.

"But he answered his father, 'Look! All these years I've been slaving for you and never disobeyed your orders. Yet you never gave me even a young goat so I could celebrate with my friends. But when this son of yours who has squandered your property with prostitutes comes home, you kill the fattened calf for him!'

"'My son,' the father said, 'you are always with me, and everything I have is yours. But we had to celebrate and be glad, because this brother of yours was dead and is alive again; he was lost and is found.'"

In this parable, the son, whom Scripture refers to as "lost," received his inheritance from his father, left his father's house, and spent his time in a far-off country squandering that inheritance. He partied, spending his money on prostitutes and all sorts of debauchery. He abandoned the values he had learned from his father. He became corrupt. Then, after his money was gone, he found himself in an economic crisis: he had no access to money, there was a famine, and no one would give him a handout. He had no place to go.

The only way the lost son was able to change his circumstances was by changing himself. The story says "he came to his senses." In the squalor of his life, in the mud and guts of a pigpen, he began to think. He saw the error of his ways and began to envision himself back at home.

His mind allowed him to imagine a brighter day.

The son's situation was so bad that he planned to beg his father to hire him as one of the servants. Anything would be better than the pigpen!

With a changed mind, the lost son picked himself up and returned home. The story tells us that his father received him without judgment and with great compassion.

Blacks in America are steeped in rich history, heritage, and culture but generally have found themselves in the country's pigpen: economically disadvantaged, disproportionately uneducated and incarcerated, and the leaders of a generation of single-parent households. Blacks are in a far-off country, so to speak; in many instances, conditions for blacks in America cannot be worse. Many segments of the black community suffer from moral decay and economic bankruptcy.

But like the lost son, the black community can survive by thinking for itself—one person at a time. Look at the circumstances in our communities today. Blacks are 13.6 percent of the population but make up 67 percent of the 21.8 million children being raised by single mothers, compared with 24 percent for whites.[1] We are the leaders in broken marriages. A disappointing 63.5 percent of blacks earned high school diplomas in the 2008-2009 Academic Year, compared with 82 percent of whites.[2] Blacks are more than 40 percent of the prison population, and more than 70 percent of black inmates were raised by single mothers, compared with 17 percent of white inmates.[3] Finally, 16 million black babies have been aborted since 1973[4]—that we know of. We have a problem. The numbers don't lie.

Notwithstanding those numbers, many blacks are conservative. Black Americans share the general belief in the benefits of hard work and are equally admiring of those who acquire wealth through it. And while they are far more supportive of government help for the needy than are whites, two-thirds of blacks share the concern that too many low-income people are dependent on government aid.[5]

Black Americans are highly patriotic (but more dubious than whites about the efficacy of military force). They are also as supportive of efforts to protect the environment and concerned about a concentration of economic power as are whites. And on issues relating to religion and morality, blacks are solidly in the conservative mainstream.[6]

So if blacks believe this way, we should behave this way. We are a conservative community. This generation must return from being lost in the far-off country and again embrace the traditional family values that made us among the greatest ethnic groups in modern history; we are descendants of kings and queens, pioneering scientists, educators, revolutionaries, and the like.

This generation of blacks must embrace policies that will lift people from their current condition, shun those policies that have kept them broke, broken, and dependent on government subsidies, and then vote accordingly. Unfortunately, Democrats, with their "progressive" agenda, have largely made empty promises and promoted bad policies.

Black Americans must come to their senses, think, return to the family values that once made our communities united and great, and match their vote with their values.

Here is what we used to say:

- Don't have sex before marriage.
- At least graduate from high school. Education is the one thing no one can ever take away from you.
- Go to church, pray, and get to know God.
- Don't have children until you get married.
- Don't shame the family name. Don't embarrass your mama.
- If you'll lie, you'll cheat; if you'll cheat, you'll kill.
- Pull up your pants, boy. You look silly.
- Respect your elders. Don't talk back to them.
- Watch your mouth!

These are among the life lessons, expressions, and experiences that produced a work ethic, pride, and a general sense of decency in the black community. While in a far-off country, the current generation has forgotten many of these values.

It is the absence of these core beliefs in everyday life and the absence of a "value vote" that propelled me to  write this book.

# Chapter 1:
## Proud Black Man

*A journey of a thousand miles must begin with a single step.*
—Chinese Proverb

Usually the first thing people notice is my cane and the "hitch in my get-along." *Basketball injury?* No. *Skiing accident?* No.

Actually, it was an attempted car repair gone bad. Or a walk-by shooting.

"Help me fix this, would you?"

The guy, about my age, my color, was bent over the open hood of a Volkswagen Jetta on the street outside my Cardinal Gardens college apartment at the edge of the USC campus in Los Angeles.

There was another guy in the driver's seat, but I didn't see him at first.

My greatest blessing, Tegra, was standing outside my apartment door, watching me return from the grocery store with a twenty-five-cent loaf of bread. She came out to meet me as I approached our apartment. It was the summer of 1987. I was in love and four days before had celebrated my twenty-second birthday.

"Fix what?" I asked the guy.

"Fix this," he said, jamming the twin barrels of a sawed-off 12-gauge shotgun against my forehead.

Time really does grind to a crawl in moments of terror. I distinctly remember everything shifting into slow motion—his words, my thoughts, Tegra's flight to safety.

"You'd better have a hundred dollars," he said.

I dropped my bag of bread and emptied what little change remained in my pockets. I was your typical starving student, living on peanut butter and jelly. I didn't have a hundred dollars, I said.

"You'd better find it," he replied.

Before I could respond, he swung the shotgun around and hit me with the rifle butt. It wasn't a hard blow, but I went down, hoping that it would be enough, that he would give up and walk away.

Instead, he stood over me, took careful aim at my head, and fired.

I'm sure he meant to shoot me in the head, but the explosive force of the shotgun firing must have thrown off his aim.

The blast hit me in the upper right thigh.

Expressionless, he looked down at me on the green grass. Then he opened the passenger door of the gold Jetta, climbed in, and they drove off.

"I was praying for angels to come, and after his car drove away and you were on the ground bleeding, they did. I saw them," said Tegra.

Who would have thought that the popular kid from West Haven, Connecticut, graduate of Notre Dame High School, and son of the famous Denver Bronco Floyd Little would find himself lying bloodied on a street in Los Angeles so far away from home?

Toni was left to do what every eighteen-year-old girl did at the time: get married and make the best of it.

Toni married Louis "Lucky" Thomas, a caring man who had always liked her. They made a go of it, giving me a presumed path to respectability.

The marriage didn't last.

Toni, one of three siblings, set out on her own without Lucky. A high school graduate, my mother worked as many jobs as necessary to make ends meet for us. After the divorce of her parents, she and my grandmother, Vera, raised me in the suburbs of West Haven, Connecticut.

My mother provided everything I needed growing up. She gave me provision and a dream.

Her provision was love, safety, religion, spirituality, fear of God, self-esteem, and education. She was a great mom. My mother kept me in church every Sunday; she paid my way through private high school and ultimately undergraduate school at the University of Southern California. I'm still trying to figure out how she did it.

Although my mother tried, she could not be a father. But she gave me a dream. You see, I always knew from as far back as I could remember who my father was. I had no memory of Lucky Thomas. I always identified with Floyd Little because that's what my mother taught me.

Floyd Little was like an action hero. Everyone knew him as the hometown hero. I was the beneficiary of that legacy from elementary school until I graduated from high school. There was always something special about being the son of a popular athlete.

The dream: "Your father loves you. One day God will bring you two together and you will know your sisters," my mother would say. Yes, I have sisters, and at the time I lived with the fact that I knew of them but they did not know of me. The dream my mother gave me was like fuel—one day I would have a dad!

In 1981, two years before graduating from high school, I met my sisters, Christy and Kyra for the first time. No one had planned it, but the forces of time made it so. One day I arrived at Grandma Little's (Dad's mom) house, and they were visiting and I didn't know it. They were excited, and I was fulfilled at last.

Since they lived in California (after growing up in Denver), it made sense that I would apply to colleges there to get to know my new family.

Although accepted to Boston College, Syracuse (Dad's alma mater), the University of Connecticut, New York University, and others, I accepted the invitation to attend the University of Southern California. My new family lived in Santa Barbara and that was close enough to Los Angeles to pursue the relationship my mother had always promised. I joined my father, his wife, Joyce, and my sisters in Santa Barbara for the summer preceding my freshman year at USC in 1983.

Oddly, my departure for the West Coast came as a surprise to my mother. Although she made preparations, purchased my one-way airline ticket, and supported the journey at every step, she didn't quite process that I was leaving home. I remember her shock the day I left.

"What? You leave today? Oh my goodness. I thought it was next week!"

I packed my bags and said good-bye to friends and my high school sweetheart, Cindy. My mother drove me to Kennedy Airport, and I never returned to Connecticut to live again.

I arrived in beautiful Santa Barbara, the kind of place I had seen only while driving through Greenwich, Connecticut. It was a beach town, a place sprinkled with local legends like Joe Cocker, steeped in Spanish heritage, and a long way from West Haven.

It was my first step to maturity and manhood. I made a huge decision to leave all that was familiar for everything unfamiliar. Although it didn't always feel comfortable, it was the best decision of my life at the time.

My family shared a great summer. I gradually came to know them all over the summer of '83, but the real depth and appreciation of relationship came only over time. As with most things, value is most often truly appreciated in the rear-view mirror of one's life.

I was back in California, a place my mother took me to visit in years past, and I was thrilled. Life was good.

By the time I was shot outside my college apartment in 1987, Dad and I had begun to build a relationship.

When word reached him of my shooting, Dad was playing in a golf tournament in West Virginia. I was supposed to be his partner, but I'd stepped on glass a few days earlier, so I had to bow out. He flew back to L.A. in a private jet provided by another of his golfing partners, the president of US Airways.

I nearly died before he arrived. The shotgun pellets severed a main artery in my leg. Most of the blood in my body had drained out through my wounds by the time I got to the hospital. I was bleeding so badly there was no time to take me to a trauma center, so the rescue squad took me to the nearest emergency room.

On the way, I was numb to the pain. I hummed an old gospel song, "Precious Lord, Take My Hand," before passing out. Then I awoke screaming in the emergency room. They claimed they'd given me pain medication. It did not seem like that to me.

I was close to death several times that night. With every code blue, Tegra, Dad, and others who kept vigil prayed that it was not me dying in those wee hours.

In the days that followed, I ballooned to 211 pounds, nearly twice my weight, because of kidney failure. I was unrecognizable. Dialysis was necessary. Hydrocephalic, my brain retained water; my eyes were swollen open. My arms and legs were tied down to prevent me from harming myself; the doctors assured my mother when she arrived that I would be brain dead and blind if I survived.

When she arrived, I was strapped to the bed, eyes covered with gauze, life support pumping my chest, breathing for me. I was a mess.

Although she didn't speak a word, when my mother entered the room, I immediately knew she was there. In my state, it is incomprehensible that I had an acute awareness of the presence of my source of life—my mother. I had peace.

Riddled with shotgun pellets, my leg swelled into a monstrous thing. Over time, my injured limb began to die. Gangrene developed in my toes, and the infection began to climb into the rest of my body. There was no choice. I had to lose the leg or die.

To save my life, they had to do the most extreme form of amputation, taking the entire leg from the hip socket. I'd been a high school track runner, always the fastest kid in my neighborhood. Now I was "different."

After months of hospitalization and rehabilitation, I was emaciated and had sunk to eighty-eight pounds. My leg muscles atrophied from a lack of movement. I had frequent flyer miles to the OR after seven surgeries. Following the amputation, doctors grafted skin from my remaining leg to repair the amputation site. The pain from skin graft operations felt like I'd been dipped in hot grease. My teeth turned purple and a bald spot was worn in the back of my head by the bed.

Through it all, Tegra, my angel, stayed by my side when many other women might have fled. I came through this trial determined to be worthy of her love.

I met Tegra on the campus of USC. She was auditioning models for the upcoming "Evening of Soul" fashion show. I fancied myself a model at the time. Well, when I laid eyes on her in October of 1985, I knew she would be my wife. Her caramel skin, light brown eyes, infectious smile, and ability to be silly with me captured my heart.

We had been dating for only a year and a half when I was shot. Her commitment and love for me when the going was so tough so early are the stuff of legend. Our partnership in life is a gift from God to me.

After dating for nearly nine years, she finally gave me her hand in marriage in 1994. We are still celebrating today.

My mother moved to Los Angeles to oversee my recovery. Her job with Amtrak allowed her that flexibility. Uncertain of my relationships (Tegra), employment, and self-esteem, she made the ultimate sacrifice. She upended her life for a year.

But I was on the fast track. After being hospitalized for four months, I checked myself out of Rancho Los Amigos Rehabilitation Center, even with a painful infection still on the mend and without a prosthetic leg. I tired of watching life pass me by. Despite all the guests, family, and friends visiting me, I was missing out.

I left the hospital in time to celebrate Thanksgiving. By the beginning of the next year, I was employed at the USC Cashier's office and with Continental Airlines. Yes, two jobs. I got around on crutches and one leg. I was back and experiencing life again.

While at Continental, I worked at the ticket counter. I checked in passengers and flung heavy baggage on the conveyer belt while on crutches. I was physically challenged, and other people knew it was a difficult adjustment. Learning to drive with only the use of my left foot was new. I was convinced, however, that getting back into the swing of things was better than being in the bed at Rancho. And it was.

"They caught him," Tegra said. Yes, while I was fighting for my life, police caught the shooter. The driver was found in the stolen Jetta and was arrested. The police, believing I would not live, scared him into thinking he would be tried for murder.

I was able to identify the shooter in a photo lineup and in a live lineup. I will never forget his face because it was frozen in time as he demanded a hundred dollars from me. He wore braids, had brown skin, and empty eyes, all at the end of a gun barrel. Unforgettable.

I also identified the driver even though I hadn't realized I saw him in the driver's seat in my subconscious.

Soon after, the shooter, Anthony Jackson, a twenty-two-year-old gang member, turned himself in to the police to avoid a manhunt for murdering a USC student.

I survived. Their crime spree that night (they stole the Jetta and tried to shoot the owner of the car) would not result in a murder charge.

They were tried in the Criminal Courts Building in downtown Los Angeles. Tegra and I both testified as to what happened that night. I got the chance to look the shooter in the face again. No remorse in those eyes.

The driver was convicted and sentenced to two years. The shooter, after a retrial, was convicted of attempted murder and sentenced to twenty-five years to life.

The horrible episode was over. I was happy to move on.

Soon after I was shot, I got a call that changed my life. Jeff Keith, an amputee who ran across California, contacted me. Jeff was a recipient of the Swim with Mike scholarship for physically challenged athletes. He was calling on behalf of the fund to offer me a scholarship to the graduate school of my choice at USC. A full ride!

This was life-altering.

After four years of trying to figure out whether I would attend business school or law school, I made it to USC's Gould School of Law. I applied every year for four years. Because of low LSAT scores, the school continued to turn me away. It was symbolic for me to pick up the pieces of my life at 'SC so I kept applying. I would not take no for an answer. Each year my LSAT scores increased. After spending two semesters at Whittier Law School and demonstrating my ability to succeed, I got the green light from USC. I was in. This was my ticket to success.

Pursuing a higher education was a life-changer. Now walking with relative comfort on a new prosthetic leg and using a cane, I was sure of myself. The shooting was becoming only a memory and not an excuse for failure or complacency. Able to take a relatively full ride on Uncle Sam with Supplemental Security Income and disability, I chose not to do so. I pursued my degree with a vengeance. My idea, since I was four years older than most of my classmates, was to open my own shop and practice music law. But I wanted to experience as many externships as I could to have a balanced perspective on the work force.

I worked for Steve Friedman, a civil litigator; I worked for the district attorney's office, handling felony preliminary hearings, and I clerked for US District Court Judge Robert M. Takasugi. My experience as a law student was rewarding.

I had an epiphany while clerking with Judge Takasugi. He gave me a chance in his chambers in a very competitive market for students. I applied to other judges, including my aunt (by marriage), Chief Justice of the District Court, Southern District of New York, Constance Baker Motley, and came up short. Ivy League students were in demand. Judge

Takasugi would contribute to helping me build my practice, but first he taught me something about myself that I did not know.

Each week, the law clerks would work on motions pending before the court. We would read both sides of the argument, research the law, and decide which side of the argument we would recommend to the judge based on the most accurate representation of the law. We would all gather once a week and present our recommendations to the judge. After working several weeks, if not months, for the judge, I was presenting my recommendation in our weekly motion meeting. After I made my eloquent presentation, as I did each week, the judge began to snicker in his polite, inoffensive way.

"What? What's so funny?" I asked. From the smiles on the faces of the others around the table, it was clear there was an inside joke that I was unaware of. I had been the topic of discussion and didn't know it.

Judge Takasugi exposed the secret. He said, "Your recommendations always take the conservative position. You're a conservative and you don't even know it."

Quietly I said, "What does that mean?" At this time in my life, I had not made an ideological choice on any issue, but somehow I had an ideological compass and it was guiding me though I didn't know it. From this point forward, I began to form an ideological identify. I asked myself, *What does it mean to be conservative? Am I one of those? Do I want to be so? What is a liberal?*

I sat in chambers pondering mind-forming questions while the shooter sat in jail pondering—what? I'm not sure.

What is striking is that we were similar in many ways. I learned that this young black man had grown up in a broken home and was raised by his grandmother, who struggled to make ends meet. Yet we had obviously chosen different paths in our lives. We were one or two decisions apart.

I was on a journey propelled by debates with a federal judge, interaction with colleagues who were Caucasian, Asian, and Hispanic, all destined to be leaders in the law, with life ahead of me: a job, a wife, the anticipation of children, a career, and liberty. An American triumph.

He, on the other hand, faced uncertainty, no job, at least not in the near future, no wife, no children (that I was aware of), no career, and certainly no liberty. An American tragedy.

I was on a thinking journey. I was living again, my own American tragedy far behind me.

Thinking is uncommon. If we just think, we have the ability to live triumphal and meaningful lives.

Mom and me (1994)

Tegra and Marc

Hawaii (2004)

# Chapter 2:

## My Politics: What I Believe

*Not to be a socialist at twenty is proof of want of heart;*
*to be one at thirty is proof of want of head.*
——*Francois Guisot*

D riving down Colorado Boulevard in Pasadena, California, minding my own business, I slowly passed to the left-hand side of a bus. I was dressed casually and not in my usual three-piece suit and tie. It was Monday, my day off.

I was in my convertible, hard top up, and the car was a little dirty from a dusty weekend.

I noticed a black man, late forties, seated and watching me from the window of the bus. That was not unusual. I find that many like my car. I did; that's why I bought it.

As I passed, I noticed his unusual behavior. He was slouched down in his seat, peering at me from the bottom corner of the bus window. He raised both hands to eye level, clenching them together with his index fingers pointed at me to form an imaginary pistol. He then motioned with his finger as if he were squeezing the trigger.

Yes, he was shooting me with his air gun! He was gunning me down on a Metro bus in the heart of Pasadena, California—the second such attempt on my life, this one more comical than the first, thank goodness!

At first, I shook my head and ignored him as I drove toward home but that dismissal didn't last for long. I began to wonder what could make me a murder target for another black man. What did he see in that moment, as I passed by, that made him feel such hatred in response to what should have been the image of himself—something to aspire to maybe, whether the car or my perceived success?

In this post-racial era with the election of President Obama, this wasn't supposed to happen anymore, right? Wasn't Obama supposed to pay our mortgages? Wasn't racism now a thing of the past? Blacks surely would rise to the occasion with one of their own now the leader of the free world, right? Instead, we had class warfare. Now I was subject to ridicule for appearing to make more than $250,000 a year and driving a car that I worked hard to purchase even if it was dirty.

Whatever choices this would-be sniper made to land himself on the bus, whether a temporary or permanent condition, he made them. I made mine.

Tegra and I married on September 3, 1994, soon after I graduated from law school. In the December that followed, I opened my law practice. I graduated, took the toughest bar exam in the nation, got married, then started a small business, all in an eight-month span. What a whirlwind! Thankfully, my California bar results came back with a "pass" that November. With $9,000 worth of loans to open my practice, I began hustling for business.

As I matured from law school student and judicial extern to attorney and husband responsible for paying all my bills, her bills, and the office bills, fiscal responsibility was knocking at my door. While I didn't become fiscally conservative overnight, the financial pressures created and fine-tuned my discipline.

I distinctly remember hearing my father say, "I work from January to July for the government and from August to December for myself." "Taxes are a bitch," he would say. That's why Dad was always a fiscal conservative; he aligned himself with the party that understood that the more money a business owner keeps in his pocket (by paying less in local, state, and federal taxes), the more prosperous he can be; the more prosperous he is, the more he reinvests to grow his business; as he reinvests and grows his business, the more jobs he creates to grow his ideas and his vision. Yes, that made sense to me and made even more sense when I began paying a 39 percent corporate tax rate to the federal government and 10 percent to the state plus self-employment tax. Paying such high taxes became a disincentive to being a business owner.

But during my awakening, I had some measure of disdain for the Republican Party because the leadership made every effort to run President Bill Clinton out of office over sex and lying. Sure, it's not good to have a liar (perjurer) or a whoremonger as a president but to distract and take down the whole country seemed a bit extreme to me.

At the time, most of my Sundays were spent worshiping at the First African Methodist Episcopal Church where the nationally known pastor, Cecil "Chip" Murray, often boomed over the pulpit and played host to presidents and corporate titans alike.

It was not uncommon to spend what seemed like a half of church service listening to elected officials or aspiring politicians tell us why they were better than their opponents. Since blacks rarely vote for Republicans, it was usually an amen chorus with no real competition for the Democratic candidate. The Republican candidates were never there—likely because they never asked to come and certainly were not invited.

Voting for the Democrat was automatic for me. Wasn't that how it was supposed to be? *Aren't they looking out for my community?* I'd say to myself.

Despite how I felt about Republican Denny Hastert, then the speaker of the House, delivering impeachment papers to the authorities over sex and lying, this period of awakening forced me to consider whether my vote matched my values.

But it wasn't until 1999 that I connected with what I now identify as socially and fiscally conservative values. The 2000 presidential election set me on a path of no return. I began to discover my values and the lines between good and evil, morality and immorality, liberal and conservative, constitutionality and unconstitutionality as they relate to the social and fiscal political issues of our day. The intersection between these areas would soon shape my ideology and who I was to become.

# The Modern-day Black Holocaust

I embarked on a deliberate exploration. The first question: pro-life or pro-choice? This question provides the single greatest dividing line between liberals and conservatives, morality and immorality, in my opinion. This is the issue many preachers choose to avoid. Apparently most believe there is reasonable disagreement. In other words, reasonable minds can disagree on abortion. I don't feel that way at all. I started examining the topic in the Bible.

Proverbs 6:16–19 tells us there are six things that God hates and that seven things are detestable to Him: haughty eyes, a lying tongue, hands that shed innocent blood, a heart that devises wicked schemes, feet that are quick to rush into evil, a false witness who pours out lies, and a man who stirs up dissension among brothers.

For the purpose of my discovery, I focused on the notion that God hates hands that shed innocent blood. Wow! This stopped me in my tracks.

I could not think of a better definition for *innocence* than an unborn child or a better definition for *shedding innocent blood* than what a doctor does to extract a fetus from a mother's womb to perform an abortion. Depending upon the procedure, the head and limbs are sucked from the womb and are identifiable as body parts as they lie in a basin. No question this is a human being as early as three weeks from conception. This is innocence that did not ask to be conceived and did not create the circumstance for that conception, whether good or bad. Such sheer innocence deserves the chance to worship its Creator.

If God hates the hands that shed innocent blood, I concluded that He hates abortion. That settled the question for me, but my awareness and interest in the issue did not end.

In my study time, I paid closer attention to the midwives in Exodus, chapter 1. Pharoah feared that the Israelites had grown to such numbers in Egypt that they would form alliances and overthrow the Egyptians.

His answer was to subject the Israelites to hard labor and then to stop their growth by killing all baby boys as they were born. His command to the Hebrew midwives Shiphrah and Puah was, "When you help the Hebrew women in childbirth and observe them on the delivery stool, if it is a boy, kill him; if it is a girl, let her live." President Obama would call this "partial birth abortion," which he favored as a state legislator in Illinois.

In 2001, 2002, and 2003, Barack Obama, then an Illinois state senator, voted against the Born-Alive Infants Protection Act[1] proposed to spare a child born alive as the result of an induced abortion. In 2003, he defended his position by saying that he would have voted for the state legislation to the extent it mirrored a federal bill signed by President

George W. Bush, but the two bills indeed contained identical language. Obama, in committee, did not support the state legislation that would have protected a born-alive fetus. The bill would have established that infants thus defined were humans with legal rights. The measure never made it to the floor; it was voted down by the Health and Human Services Committee, which Obama chaired.

But the Hebrew women feared God, the Bible tells us, and they did not do what the king of Egypt told them to do. They let the boys live. I believe they understood how God felt about shedding innocent blood.

Similarly today, most women and men who order the murder of their children do so out of fear, just like the king. They fear the ruin of their lives: "I won't finish school." "What will they think of me?" "I can't afford a baby." Just like the king, many of us are narcissistic and simply don't value any life but our own.

A colleague recently argued her case to me for being pro-choice. Her reasoning was that the fetus was a parasite—yes, a parasite she called it—and that she could decide at any moment to kill the parasite since it was feeding on her body.

Many feel as she does, and such people have gone astray. No use in arguing with a completely carnal mind. I gave her no argument. She had no biblical foundation, and I didn't have the time to pour it.

In making a decision about abortion, the issue's history should not be ignored. Before the *Roe v. Wade* decision was handed down in 1973, white women were responsible for having 80 percent of all illegal abortions.

Since *Roe v. Wade,* the abortion rate among black women is five times that of white women in the United States, according to the Guttmacher Institute.[2] Black women (15-44) are responsible for 40.2% of all abortions in the United States.[3]

But there was a long, dark history before *Roe v. Wade* that led to the genocide in the black community we see today. The efforts of the American Eugenics Society and its founder, Francis Galton, funded in large part in later years by the Carnegie Corporation of New York and the Rockefeller Foundation, began right after the Emancipation Proclamation took effect. The agenda of the white elites was based on fear and driven by economics and racism.

Every aspect of the American economy was invested in the slave trade, so first and foremost, there was a general fear of retribution by the four million freed slaves. The North feared a massive migration. White elites also feared that freed slaves would flood the economic system with new costs for welfare, medical care, and education. These burdens on society would result in higher taxes. So the people who had been enslaved for hundreds of years were now an economic burden after their freedom. The elites also feared that intermarriage would destroy the purity of the white race. Finally, they feared an increase in crime and the prison population.

The first response was colonization (shipping the Negro back to Africa), but the idea didn't have wide support. Then the white and wealthy schemed to wipe out the Negro race in America. Eugenics was the answer.

Eugenics was a movement to shrink the future Negro populations by controlling the birth rate. Drastic measures were attempted in eugenics.

Eugenics failed over time but not for lack of trying. The movement imposed sterilization on black people by the thousands. Forced sterilization was done on girls as young as ten, although the practice in Maryland and other states faced constitutional challenges.

Adolf Hitler mimicked the American eugenics playbook and exterminated Jews. Eventually, eugenics slithered below ground after getting a bad name from Nazi Germany. The word *eugenics* became unpopular the world over; the movement died, but the architects made a shift.

Reducing the growth of the black population around the world, but especially in America, was still the goal—by any means necessary.

Negative eugenics followed. The idea was to create an environment that would convince blacks to limit the number of their children, in effect to accept "race suicide." This movement was carried out by crusaders like Margaret Sanger, the founder of the American Birth Control League.

In 1922, Sanger said that "we are paying for and even submitting to the dictates of an ever-increasing, unceasingly spawning class of human beings who never should have been born at all."[4]

In 1942, the American Birth Control League changed its name to Planned Parenthood. The organization is now the largest operator of abortion clinics in the United States and is still obsessed with race and eugenics.

Now, instead of the Carnegie Corporation and the Rockefeller Foundation providing the largest support for the extermination of the black population, the American taxpayer is the largest supporter of abortions, just ahead of America's titans of business, Melinda and Bill Gates and Warren Buffett.

Among the first anti-abortion groups during the 1960s civil rights era were the Black Panthers and the Nation of Islam. They spoke out against birth control and abortion.

"Abortion is genocide,"[5] warned the Rev. Jesse Jackson.

Under the banner of protecting women's reproductive rights, many were willing to sell out the community in exchange for political support. Our black politicians today support the Planned Parenthood agenda, and black people line up daily to murder their children.

The wool has officially been pulled over the eyes of the black community. Evidence: Planned Parenthood's past president was Faye Wattleton, a black woman.

Now abortion, previously decried by most civil rights activists as genocide, has mysteriously and quietly become a question of a "woman's right to choose."

"The federal government's economic stimulus package should include a large increase for population control. This would save the federal government from having to pay for the health care and education costs of poor children," Nancy Pelosi, then speaker of the House, told ABC News on January 25, 2009. Pelosi has a 100 percent approval rating from Planned Parenthood. Sounds like she is singing the same song as those who feared the impact of the Negro on the US economy in the nineteenth century. Coincidence?

We are asleep, and like sheep we have gone astray.

Women and men must seek the aid of crisis pregnancy clinics that routinely respond to unplanned pregnancies with multiple resources for couples that may include housing, financial assistance, parenting classes, and adoption referrals. Murder should never be the answer to an unplanned or unwanted pregnancy.

# The Question of Capital Punishment

In defining my views on the social issues of our day, I had to come to terms with my feelings not only on abortion but on capital punishment. Should the state be allowed to take a life?

If the law includes rigorous due process and equal protection, I favor the death penalty.

I struggled with the proven fallibility of the government and the possibility of convicting and sentencing to death an innocent man or woman. In light of the likelihood that at some point an innocent person will be convicted and sentenced to death, is life in prison the better alternative to the death penalty? When balanced against the need for a strong deterrent against murder, I think not. Studies show that the death penalty actually saves lives. They demonstrate time and time again a link between executions and a reduced murder rate.

Conversely, commuted sentences, death-row removals, and moratoriums on executions appear to increase the incidence of murder.

On the other hand, until recently, users of crack cocaine, who are usually black, were given mandatory five-year jail sentences for possessing five grams while users of powder cocaine, who are usually white, had to possess five hundred grams to get the same mandatory five years. In the same way, blacks have been disproportionately sentenced to the death penalty. But this does not mean that blacks have been treated unfairly. There is little evidence to suggest they have.

And I cannot ignore the Rand Corporation's independent studies that reveal the death penalty is driven by the characteristics of the crime and not by race.

America executes murderers because it hates evil. That sets us apart in a unique way, one that I support.

I also turned to the Scriptures. What does God say about the death penalty?

There are many passages in both the Old and New Testaments that support a biblical principle of capital punishment. I find Genesis 9:5–6 important to gain a biblical understanding of the death penalty and justice.

"For your own lifeblood I will surely require a reckoning: from every animal I will require it and from human beings, each one for the blood of another, I will require a reckoning for human life. Whoever sheds the blood of a human, by a human shall that person's blood be shed; for in his own image God made mankind."

God instituted capital punishment in the Old Testament, and it was never repudiated in the New Testament by Jesus or the apostles.

God believes in the sanctity of human life, and to take a life is an attack on God Himself. He requires payment for that. An eye for an eye.

## Same-sex Marriage

The third leg to the triad stool of taboo issues is same-sex marriage— the new moral wedge issue. It is a religious issue, in my opinion, that has become politicized. It is a religious issue because with the creation of humanity, described in Genesis 1:1, God established marriage as a sacred covenant between one man and one woman. I choose to follow the biblical example.

(While many argue a lack of fairness on this issue because they were born gay and should be accorded the same treatment as heterosexual couples, I make no judgment as to whether a person is born a homosexual. I don't know the truth of the matter despite what science may pretend to prove. However, my interpretation of the Bible proscribes the practice of homosexuality, notwithstanding counter interpretations by many theologians.).

All across our nation, the same-sex marriage agenda is championed by a minority in our society hell-bent on forcing those of us who are not gay, lesbian, bisexual, or transgendered to alter centuries-old traditions.

Paula Ettelbrick, former policy director of the National Center for Lesbian Rights, recently wrote, "Being queer is more than setting up house, sleeping with a person of the same gender, and seeking state approval for doing so … Being queer means pushing the parameters of sex, sexuality, and family; and in the process, transforming the very fabric of society."

Yes, the homosexual agenda (secular and religious) attempts to transform our view of traditional marriage joining those decay-causing movements that took prayer out of public schools, tried to take God out of the Pledge of Allegiance, banned the Ten Commandments from the courthouse, and are sliding "In God We Trust" off of American currency.

In an attempt to gain the support of the black community and others, activists call the gay agenda the civil rights issue of our day.

They cry "civil rights" and "unfair treatment," but this is not a civil rights issue, and claiming so is offensive to those—namely blacks and women—who have obvious immutable and physical traits for which they have been discriminated against as a group.

Those who pander to the notion that the same-sex agenda is akin to the civil rights issue of the '60s or the women's suffrage movement should be ashamed. It should not even be mentioned in the same sentence. The causes of the discriminatory experiences faced by blacks and women verses gays are not comparable, assuming the gay lifestyle is a choice.

Whether the question turns on the Bible or any particular state constitution, marriage has always been defined as between one man and one woman. The majority of Americans would like to keep it that way, which should not be confused with the attempt to eliminate the brutal treatment that blacks and women experienced as a result of their color or gender.

In 2008, blacks resoundingly supported Proposition 8 in California. Seven in ten blacks voted to overturn a California Supreme Court decision that legalized same-sex marriage.[6]

Let's not pass legislation to make same-sex marriage socially acceptable. That goes too far.

The line should be drawn at a contract that affords same-sex partners any and all rights that may be contained in a contract. We are all free to contract with each other on any legal basis. The social contract should be enforceable with respect to health care, estate planning issues, access as prescribed by each partner, and the like. Federal provisions should also be made to extend retirement benefits to any beneficiary, including a same-sex partner. This type of agreement does not offend and would allow each of us to manage our affairs as we see fit.

I stand for and with my gay and lesbian friends. I love them dearly. However, I do not support same-sex marriage.

# Immigration

If I'm in line at the McDonald's drive-thru, it's really busy, and I've had a longer- than-usual wait, is it okay for someone to cut into the line ahead of me—or should he wait his turn?

Another analogy: As comedian and radio talk-show host Dennis Miller often says, "What's wrong with asking who is staying in my house? If I have a house guest, it's fair to want to know who you are." It's not racist or bigoted to ask the question, no matter what anyone says. Sorry. Just makes sense.

I do not intend to offend by comparing what has become a national legal and humanitarian crisis to the drive-thru at McDonald's or being a house guest. I understand and appreciate the motivation of fathers and mothers to make a better life in America. I do not intend to diminish anyone's humanity or our obligation to treat everyone, including the illegal alien, with decency and respect. For me, it's about the law of the land, and politics has gotten in the way of enforcing it.

Democrats and Republicans alike have made immigration a political issue. Democrats want to grant illegal aliens (that's right, not "undocumented workers") citizenship in exchange for what they believe will be a group of guaranteed voters. It is estimated that there are nearly twelve million illegal aliens, mostly from Mexico, in the United States. Some say the number is closer to twenty million. That would be a big gain for the Democrats if they pass immigration reform and amnesty.

If recent Democratic proposals to provide driver's licenses to the illegal workers pass, who needs citizenship? The illegal worker would be able to vote with a driver's license alone. And if recent efforts succeed in California, a library card will suffice.

While Democrats argue, "Let's bring the illegal worker out of the shadows [by throwing open our nation's borders]," they ignore the exploitation and victimization of women and children, human trafficking and the sex trade, kidnapping, drug trafficking, and the weapons dealing facilitated by unfettered migration to the promised land. Where is the compassion for those illegal aliens who are constantly abused by this underground capitalistic border industry?

Republicans have their own hand in the pot. Many want comprehensive immigration reform, a code name for amnesty, because they claim illegal workers willingly do jobs Americans will not perform. This keeps labor costs low and increases net profits, but that's no reason to support breaking the law.

Immigration is not a political or humanitarian issue but rather a legal issue, pure and simple. Virtually no other nation allows the entry of want-to-be-workers or citizens without documentation. For example, Mexico has the most stringent immigration laws, yet it chastised us for the Arizona law that sought to stem the tide of illegal immigration by enforcing the letter of the federal law. Here are snippets of Mexico's General Law on Population[7]:

- Foreigners are admitted into Mexico "according to their possibilities of contributing to national progress."
- Immigration officials must "ensure" that "immigrants will be useful elements for the country and that they have the necessary funds for their sustenance" and for their dependents. (Article 34)
- Foreigners may be barred from the country if their presence upsets "the equilibrium of the national demographics," if they are deemed detrimental to "economic or national interests," if they do not behave like good citizens in their own country, if they have broken Mexican laws, and if "they are not found to be physically or mentally healthy." (Article 37)
- The secretary of governance may "suspend or prohibit the admission of foreigners when he determines it to be in the national interest." (Article 38)

As for foreigners with fake papers or those who enter the country under false pretenses:

- Foreigners with fake immigration papers may be fined or imprisoned. (Article 116)
- Foreigners who sign government documents "with a signature that is false or different from that which he

29

normally uses" are subject to fine and imprisonment. (Article 116)

Foreigners who fail to obey the rules will be fined, deported, and/ or imprisoned as felons:

- Foreigners who fail to obey a deportation order are to be punished. (Article 117)
- Foreigners who are deported from Mexico and attempt to reenter the country without authorization can be imprisoned for up to ten years. (Article 118)
- Foreigners who violate the terms of their visas may be sentenced to up to six years in prison (Articles 119, 120, and 121). Foreigners who misrepresent the terms of their visas while in Mexico—such as working without a permit—can also be imprisoned.

Under Mexican law, illegal immigration is a felony. The General Law on Population says,

- "A penalty of up to two years in prison and a fine of three hundred to five thousand pesos will be imposed on the foreigner who enters the country illegally." (Article 123)
- Foreigners with legal immigration problems may be deported from Mexico instead of being imprisoned. (Article 125)
- Foreigners who "attempt against national sovereignty or security" will be deported. (Article 126)

Mexicans who help illegal aliens enter the country are themselves considered criminals under the law:

- A Mexican who marries a foreigner with the sole objective of helping the foreigner live in the country is subject to up to five years in prison. (Article 127)
- Shipping and airline companies that bring undocumented foreigners into Mexico will be fined. (Article 132)

Yet Mexico has the gall to chastise America generally and Arizona specifically about its immigration policy. America is at war, and the back door is open. In addition, illegal aliens commit their fair share of violent and nonviolent felonies. Virtually anyone can walk across our porous northern and southern borders. It's ridiculous.

Meanwhile, our nation is burdened with noncitizens contributing to traffic on the roads, crowding our emergency rooms, where getting care is increasingly impossible in a reasonable amount of time, and filling our classrooms, where we now must offer English as a second language, all on the US taxpayer's dime.

We are giving away our nation and catering to those who thumb their noses at our laws while politicians curry favor to stay in power. Who are they to decide what laws to enforce and what laws to ignore? Sanctuary cities, such as San Francisco, brazenly fail to arrest and deport illegal aliens who are caught doing crimes, while Americans caught in similar situations are locked up.

I lived in Santa Barbara during the summer of 1983 before attending USC. While we were in our backyard cooking over the Fourth of July holiday, we heard a great crash in front of the house. We all rushed out to see what the commotion was about.

We spotted and stopped a migrant worker climbing out of the car he was driving. It had plowed into all three of our family cars parked in front. He had made it to the trunk from which he was extricating his getaway bicycle.

We held him and called the police. He spoke no English.

When a police officer arrived, he had a chat with the worker. Apparently, the officer spoke Spanish. After less than five minutes, the worker put his bicycle back in the trunk and drove away as we stood by in awe and wonder.

Our mouths were agape!

The officer said, "They pick the oranges up here. You have insurance, don't you?"

So not only do these immigrants break the law to get here, but they are allowed to violate our civil liberties when they arrive. Something is very wrong with this picture.

This nation is out of control.

Black Americans are disproportionately affected by the great migration from Mexico. Illegal aliens are displacing blacks from the work force. The low-paying jobs that blacks worked as cooks, cleaners, drivers, domestic help, and the like are now filled by Mexicans for pennies on the dollar along with the not-so-low paying jobs for contractors and construction workers. No one is complaining about that disproportionate effect on the black community. If someone is complaining, it is not loud enough. Hello?

On June 17, 2011, President Obama's memo to John Morgan, director of Immigration and Customs Enforcement, discourages deportation of illegal aliens who agree to enlist in the US military, enroll in college, or are pregnant or nursing. It is essentially an act of amnesty. The DREAM Act called for essentially the same thing. That bill failed to pass Congress on two separate occasions, so our president simply passed it on his own through the back door, circumventing the will of the legislative branch. Is that the way our government is supposed to work? I thought Congress makes the laws and the executive branch is supposed to enforce them. What happened here? Then in response to the failed DREAM Act, in June 2012 the president passed by executive order that illegal immigrants under 30 years old who have been in the US since they were 16 and have lived in the US for at least 5 years are eligible for deferred action which amounts to a suspension of deportation. This group would then be eligible for work permits.

In addition, financial aid for college is often provided to the illegal alien depending upon the state. Several states—Texas, California, New York, Utah, Illinois, Washington, Nebraska, New Mexico, Maryland (community colleges), Oklahoma, Wisconsin, and Kansas —have passed laws providing in-state tuition benefits to illegal aliens who have attended high school in the state for three or more years. Similar legislation is pending in Florida, Hawaii, Massachusetts, Minnesota, New Hampshire, New Jersey, North Carolina, Oregon, South Carolina, Tennessee, and Virginia. (Connecticut also passed such a law, but the governor vetoed it.) The Nevada system of higher education does not consider immigration status for in-state tuition, but does require it for a state-sponsored scholarship. Some schools in Georgia provide in-state tuition benefits to illegal aliens. The Texas law also allows illegal aliens to receive state student financial aid.

These state laws attempt to circumvent federal law simply by failing to ask students whether they are in the US legally. (The California law, A.B. 540, requires students to submit an affidavit that they have filed an application to legalize their immigration status or intend to file an application as soon as they are eligible to do so. California doesn't even attempt to maintain the fiction that the school is unaware of the student's immigration status.) States also circumvent the law by basing eligibility for in-state tuition on attendance at or graduation from an in-state high school and not on state residence. [8]

But what about the migrant worker? The Mexican worker is being exploited. Why is it all right to be paid substandard wages in America? Few are complaining about the exploitation of the migrant worker. What is going on? Somebody fix this, please.

Here is the answer. Secure the border—for real. This means more Border Patrol agents, multilayered fencing, and electronic surveillance. Create a guest worker program that gets qualified workers into the country in a manageable way; then make it a major crime for employers to hire illegal workers and start locking up chief executives for violating the law. They would immediately stop filling jobs with illegal workers.

Those who could not be hired for lack of a work visa would deport themselves. Only then will we return to a normal flow of controlled immigration.

This great country was built on legal immigration. There is no reason to stop now. Operative word: *legal.*

# The American Dream

Everyone in America has the choice to dream. If you dare to dream, in America, your dream can come true with education, hard work, and acceptance of personal responsibility.

Achieving the American dream revolves around how one defines the role of the individual against the role of government. The American dream is simple. It's the finest idea but hard to achieve anywhere else in the world. That's why almost everyone wants to live here. This idea says that an individual can dream and create his own destiny, to succeed or not, to pursue happiness or not, to build a business or not, to have a family or not, to worship God or not. It is an idea built around individual choice and is realized only when government stays out of the way.

The American dream, no matter your race, has three essential ingredients: self-reliance (strengthened by hard work and personal responsibility), the free-market system (also known as capitalism), and liberty. With these three principles at work in unison, the American dream remains vibrant.

The first of these—self-reliance—is the cornerstone of the philosophy of the great black American thinker Booker T. Washington.

Washington, the originator of black conservatism and founder of Tuskegee University in Tuskegee, Alabama, had three important themes: education, self-reliance, and entrepreneurship. He believed that these principles were the tools by which former slaves could achieve freedom and prosperity at the dawn of the twentieth century. This holds true even today.

Like his mentor, Frederick Douglass, a former slave and abolitionist, Washington believed that if whites would just leave blacks alone, they could take care of themselves.

After Reconstruction (1865–77), Washington advocated education for blacks because the former slaves were illiterate; it was illegal to teach slaves to read. His first priority was education. After raising money from the white elite to found Tuskegee in 1881, he said, "The ambition to secure an education was most praiseworthy and encouraging."[9] His classrooms were filled day and night, with some students as old as seventy.

Nearly a hundred years later, blacks under South Africa's apartheid system believed similarly. The motto of the young freedom fighters was, "Freedom first, education second." Inherent in this motto was the importance of getting an education after breaking free from their white oppressors.

Washington understood that education for the emancipated slave in America was the road to self-reliance. Tuskegee focused on training men and women in construction and farming and other practical skills, with less emphasis on liberal arts education. These practical skills proved to be a bridge to the mainstream and to self-reliance.

I recently saw a film titled *Waiting for Superman*. I admit that I cried during the movie.

The film is about the education system in the US generally, but it highlights the Washington, D.C., Los Angeles, and New York school districts and the young students vying for spots in the handful of charter schools available in their areas. The parents, mostly single, and their kids are praying to get out of the schools killing their futures. Our schools are failing our kids on a massive level. Thousands upon thousands are attending class with teachers who are not paid based on performance but based on their membership in the teachers union. This is an American tragedy.

The movie depicts the failing system that matriculates students from elementary school to middle school to high school without the basic ability to read and do arithmetic. Most, if not all, of the students trapped in these low-performing schools are minorities. The union stands in the way of progress.

The American Federation of Teachers fights against reform that would require teachers to produce results— passing scores, proficiency in math, proficiency in reading and grammar—to get merit pay. Instead, one hidden camera shows students playing craps in the back of the room while the teacher reads a newspaper. This is happening all across our nation today. Where is Superman? Who will remind our teachers to act as though education is the conduit to the future—the American dream—not merely the means to a paycheck?

I want teachers to be paid commensurate to the importance of their job in our society. Conversely, poor-performing teachers should not be protected by behemoth unions that fail our students and consequently destroy our nation's future.

We must recognize the decay in our education system. While private and charter schools are not the only solution, they are picking up the slack. I had the pleasure of being a co-founding board member of Crown Preparatory Academy, a public charter middle school in Los Angeles, with Laura McGowan-Robinson. Laura, a former teacher from Chicago, decided to do something about the education problem in the inner city. By the end of its first year, Crown Prep had surpassed the performance of long-established public schools in the immediate area, and its scholars are excelling in every subject. We need more Laura's and more Crown Preps in our communities.

Finally, Washington rightly taught entrepreneurship as a way to build an economic foundation in the aftermath of failed Reconstruction policies. Blacks gained a significant presence in Congress, more than at any time since. But those political inroads failed to produce freedom and prosperity for the entire community. Washington favored a grassroots approach to independence. He encouraged thousands of blacks to look to the needs of the community and build businesses to meet those needs. He personally connected many to wealthy white investors. He understood that without economic independence as individuals and as a community, blacks had no alternative but to rely on the generosity of whites and the government, which had been historically untrustworthy.

His 1901 autobiography, *Up From Slavery*, the first best-selling book by a black author, fully explores these three principles. Washington picked up the mantle of Frederick Douglass and became the voice and leader of black America.

Sadly, his philosophy was overshadowed (and nearly forgotten) because of his antagonist, W.E.B. Du Bois. Du Bois argued that Washington's philosophy could not achieve the desired results without full political rights. He believed Washington was soft on segregation and soft on criticizing white-on-black violence; he also believed Washington was opposed to higher education because he promoted education in the trades. Washington became known as an Uncle Tom.

With the publication of Du Bois's book *The Souls of Black Folk*, blacks became divided—one camp loyal to Washington and the other to Du Bois. With the support of white philanthropists and the National Association for the Advancement of Colored People (NAACP), Du Bois's philosophy is widely followed today, while blacks still struggle for economic independence and limited, if any, political power.

History is a funny rear-view mirror. Washington understood that with self-reliance created by education, the black community could sustain itself. He had a practical plan. He built institutions to carry it out, while his opponents had no plan at all. Instead of attacking whites in public, he quietly worked and paid whites to spy on other whites and hired lawyers to fight the Jim Crow laws—strategies unheard of among blacks during that time. He was a clever fox.

Today, those organizations that make political access the focus, the Du Bois way, march the black community into the pits of despair because they still have no practical plan.

I hang on to one of Washington's phrases. He said, "The Negro must own his own land, milk his own cow, and hitch his own mule to his own wagon." That thought still applies to us today.

The second leg of the American dream is the free-market system. Capitalism creates more wealth and opportunities than any other economic model. "[It] is an intricate system of voluntary economic, social and cultural interactions that are motivated by the desires and needs of the individual and the community." [10]

In the United States, each individual has the choice to get up every day, enter the free-market system (whether as a factory worker, baker, or small-business owner), apply hard work, contribute to the free market, and achieve his dream.

Contributing to the free market is like being a participant in an assembly line. Each individual has a part to play, and if it is played with integrity, the entire community advances.

This system has proven to be the best economic model, one that allows us all to create our own sense of being, our own value based upon our ability to achieve. In *Liberty and Tyranny*, Mark Levin refers to this as our "private property," the material value created from the intellectual and/or physical labor of the individual, which may take the form of income, real property, or intellectual property. This appreciation of private property is critical to understanding the free market.

As the federal government taxes or regulates private property (income, real property, or intellectual property) to pay for entitlement programs or arbitrary government spending, the worth of our labor declines. I have a finite number of hours to work in my lifetime. I desire to work as much as I can to pass on a legacy to my grandchildren (generational wealth). The more the federal government taxes my labor, the longer I have to work to achieve my goals each year to benefit those who will come after me. The more I get taxed, the more years I will need in my plan and the less secure my family will be over time. Eventually, I will run out of time, and my survivors will be left to toil as I have on the government's treadmill to nowhere.

As an example, at a combined 50 percent tax rate, I work from January 1 to June 30 to pay the government and from July 1 to December 31 to earn enough to meet my goals for my family and our future.

As the federal government increases my taxes, let's say to 60 percent, I am working longer days and weeks to pay my taxes and I have less time during the year to meet my annual goals.

The more this continues, the more I work for the government and the closer I get to being a slave.

This tax scheme undermines the success of the best economic system the world has ever known simply because our government cannot control its spending.

Its legalized stealing and an intricate, involuntary economic system motivated purely by the desires and needs of hapless federal bureaucrats.

The fallacy of taxing income at exorbitant levels is that the federal government believes it knows best how to spend the taxpayer's money. Rather, the individual knows better how to make and spend what he earns from the labor of his hands and to provide for his family than does the bureaucrat, who sees the taxpayer as one large source of revenue for the government as opposed to an individual with his own plans.

Our economic system should be unfettered and supported by the federal government as a way to promote the creation of private property and as a necessary means of achieving the American dream.

Finally, there is the concept of liberty, the third leg to the American dream. Ah yes, freedom. The desire to be free from oppression motivated so many of my sisters and brothers in South Africa to march, in many instances to their deaths, against apartheid; the desire to free millions from bondage motivated the great abolitionists Harriet Tubman and Frederick Douglass; and the desire to end the lynching of black men, women, and children in the Jim Crow South motivated the great men and women of the civil rights era. Freedom, called *liberty* in the Declaration of Independence, is crucial to accomplishing the American dream but fades daily from the American landscape in the twenty-first century.

A small and limited federal government produces a garden where liberty flourishes.

The United States Constitution is just one of the intended safeguards of this idea. It provides that "The powers not delegated to the United States by the Constitution, nor prohibited by it to the States, are reserved to the States respectively, or to the people."

When the leaders of the day follow the intent of the Founding Fathers, the Constitution works and provides for a limited federal government. In the system known as federalism, the federal, state, and local governments work in balance, each playing a role in American life; the federal government's role was limited to a few important areas: national defense, immigration, issuing currency, raising revenue to operate national government, overseeing foreign relations, and resolving conflicts between states, as a few examples. The federal government retained exclusive control in these areas. Everything else was intended to fall to the states.

When the federal government gets it right, it gets out of the way and does not create massive entitlement programs like Social Security, Medicare, and Medicaid that require more and more of the taxpayers' income to fund year after year.

But progressives like Franklin D. Roosevelt have twisted the Constitution to create a nanny state from which many of the poor-in-mind have been spawned. This has increased government largess, bringing greater dependence on the dole and ultimately less liberty for those who want to work for a living. It is not fair and is un-American.

The entitlement programs of the 1930s are now broken, in part because the federal government is not the best vehicle to run retirement or health care. We have not learned the lessons of our past and are creating more government programs that require greater government spending year after year. These affairs are best left to the individual and the private sector where personal responsibility and competition govern.

For example, Social Security, the largest government program in the world, began as a one-lump-sum retirement program and expanded to a family-based economic system that is now broken. Created under Franklin Roosevelt, the program, now 37 percent of all government expenditures and 7 percent of gross domestic product, projects massive deficits in years to come because of government inertia. Meanwhile, we borrow and borrow to make up for the mismanagement. This is classic government. Instead of fixing the problem, it is left to the next generation, and the system is more broken at every turn.

Similarly, the government should not be in health care. The federal government can't run the Postal Service efficiently as evidenced by that agency's failure against the growth of Federal Express and the United Parcel Service. Why give it the burden of the health care system beyond what currently exists (the Department of Veterans Affairs, for example)? While many of our seniors, veterans, and poor certainly benefit from government-provided health care and insurance, it is unwise to expand the system beyond these broken programs to cover the phantom fifty million uninsured Americans (a fake number since many are illegal aliens and others who can afford insurance but simply don't want it).

If the government really wanted to fix the health care industry, it would provide an environment that reduces costs. We can drive down costs by limiting the need for doctors to practice defensive medicine. In other words, we should fight the trial lawyers by punishing frivolous lawsuits that require doctors to order every test known to man to avoid malpractice claims that drive up the costs of treatment. Another approach would be to make premiums competitive by allowing Americans to purchase insurance across state lines, as they can with auto insurance. Currently, health insurance is purchased on a state-by-state basis and is generally employment based, which limits competition to those companies within a state, thus driving up costs. Coverage should also be portable so that when an employee changes jobs and moves out of state, insurance is not lost.

Under the Patient Protection and Affordable Care Act, also called ObamaCare which was challenged and declared constitutional by the US Supreme Court in June 2012, the administration banned restrictions on those with pre-existing conditions among other things but none leading to reduced costs in care that I can tell. The act is subject to repeal or defunding if the Republicans every get the votes in the Senate.

Notwithstanding ObamaCare, if these simple measures would indeed make health insurance more affordable, why wouldn't the federal government focus on these areas? Good question. I believe we have reached a point in our history where our liberty is no longer the goal of some of our leaders. They are more interested in how many of us they can force into a system of dependence like universal health care. The more control, as with health care, the government has over our lives, the closer we are to socialism. Socialism is a system whereby control of capital and the means of production and distribution rests with the government. According to Karl Marx, socialism is the logical step from capitalism to communism. When government gets too big, it becomes socialistic by default. Then what? We must tread lightly.

Some want to perpetuate the failed entitlement programs of our past that pour more and more Americans onto the government dole, making each one more and more dependent on the government.

The Obama administration provided an unprecedented extension of unemployment benefits from the normal twenty-six weeks, to thirty-nine weeks, and now to ninety-nine weeks, bringing the length of time an unemployed worker could draw 50 percent salary to nearly two years. Imagine that—sit home and collect half your pay for nearly two years. If the national unemployment rate remains high, the federal government will likely try to extend benefits even further. The unemployment rate under the Obama administration soared as high as 9.1 percent. This does not account for those no longer looking or those no longer eligible for unemployment benefits, which means the national average is much higher. It's also of note that the unemployment rate among blacks is higher than for any other ethnicity. As of August 2011, it climbed to 16.7 percent while it fell to 8 percent for whites![11]

Replacing paychecks with unemployment benefits for extended periods of time is not the role of government. When government just distributes checks in response to a downturn, it creates an unhealthy dependence that diminishes creativity and innovation, ultimately destroying production and our nation's future. This redistribution of wealth does not work. Government must not treat the symptom of unemployment but must treat the cause.

Where private businesses are failing, the government can and should provide tax credits (like an employment tax holiday) that allow small-business owners to pay less in taxes for a period of time. This keeps money in the pocket of the small-business entrepreneur, who will by nature reinvest in the business. When that investment works, it creates momentum in that business, which leads to growth and more jobs.

The federal government must not treat the symptom of unemployment by feeding the worker but must treat the cause by lifting the burden from the small-business owner, who is the economic engine of this country.

When the federal government tries to solve the problems of the individual by throwing money around, the result is oppression. Some of the greatest civilizations have done that and have failed. Great Britain and most recently Greece are primary examples. Government cannot spend its way out of its troubles. It must let the individual loose to create, it must let the free-market system work by fostering an atmosphere of competition, and it must embrace the idea of liberty as a necessary ingredient to prosperity for the individual and the nation. This makes the American dream possible but requires true leadership at the top.

# Chapter 3:

## From Republican to Democrat: The Black Political Journey

*If the Negroes—numbering one-eighth of the population of these United States—would only cast their votes in the interest of the Democratic Party, all open measures [of violence] against them would be immediately suspended and their rights as American citizens recognized. But ... I can only say that we love freedom more—vastly more—than slavery; consequently we hope to keep clear of the Democrats!*
*—United States Representative Joseph Hayne Rainey,*
*black Republican from South Carolina, 1871*

All voting black Americans supported the Republican Party after being emancipated from slavery in 1865. But tactical decisions made by the GOP years later combined with the masterful and covert schemes of the southern Democrats led blacks away from the party of the Great Emancipator, Abraham Lincoln. Black Americans slowly migrated from the Republican Party and have remained loyal to the Democrats ever since.

The history of black Americans began in 1619 with the arrival of the first slaves in Jamestown, Virginia. The transatlantic slave trade—the *maafa* (holocaust), among the largest forced migrations in human history—was responsible for transporting more than twelve million Africans to North and South America from central and west Africa. The *maafa* involved four continents, spanned four centuries, and was among the greatest human tragedies, affecting an entire race of people in the Americas and second only to the much larger slave trade from Africa benefiting Muslim countries for ten centuries. The condition of the black slave, deliberately trained to be inferior to whites, left its mark on the American political system.

The political history of blacks in America began with the writing of the Constitution in 1787 although the legal history began in the seventeenth century when laws were passed that directly and indirectly affected the status and freedom of slaves and their children. (Beginning in the 1660s, the colonies legalized slavery and fashioned laws to make slaves and their children slaves for life and to fine those who harbored runaways.)

# The Constitution is Not a Racist Document

The US Constitution is often referred to as a racist document primarily because of its authors and because of the three-fifths clause. Much has been made of this clause. It is often taught that the Constitution is a pro-slavery document and racist against blacks. That's a lie.

Article 1, Section 2, embodying the three-fifths clause reads:

Representatives and direct Taxes shall be apportioned among the several States which may be included within this Union, according to their respective Numbers, which shall be determined by adding to the whole Number of free Persons, including those bound to Service for a Term of Years, and excluding Indians not taxed, three fifths of all other Persons.

A study of the background of this clause reveals that it dealt only with representation in Congress and not with the worth of a black man or woman. That's right—it has nothing to do with a black man or woman being worth only three-fifths of a human.

Under the Constitution, a state would receive one representative to Congress for every thirty thousand inhabitants. The southern states saw this as a chance to strengthen pro-slavery representation in Congress, so they decided to count the slaves as inhabitants instead of property, as they had done historically.[1] This scheme would have given the southern states more representatives in Congress, allowing them to expand and sustain the slave trade. As an example, 50 percent of the inhabitants of South Carolina were slaves,[2] which would have given that state disproportionate representation had Congress adopted the southern scheme. (The South's desire to expand the slave trade to new territories and to secede from the North was so strong that it would eventually lead to the Civil War.)

The anti-slavery northern founders rejected this scheme to increase the power of the southern slave owners. While these abolitionists wanted free blacks counted, they stood firm on limiting the political power of the South and rejected counting slaves as inhabitants for the purpose of representation in the Congress. In fact, free blacks in the North and South were extended the full rights of citizens and regularly voted.[3]

Freed slave and abolitionist Frederick Douglass made the determination for himself after studying the Constitution. He said,

The Constitution is a glorious liberty document. Read its preamble; consider its purposes. Is slavery among them? Is it at the gateway? Or is it in the temple? It is neither ... If the Constitution were intended to be, by its framers and adopters, a slaveholding instrument, why neither slavery, slaveholding, nor slave can anywhere be found in it? Now, take the Constitution according to its plain reading and I defy the presentation of a single pro-slavery clause in it. On the other hand, it will be found to contain principles and purposes entirely hostile to the existence of slavery.[4]

The three-fifths clause (or 60 percent of the southern states' slave population) was the final compromise. Instead of thirty thousand slaves accounting for one state representative to Congress, it would take fifty thousand to get an additional representative.

In other words, the clause that many teach to be dehumanizing pro-slavery language is just the opposite; it is an anti-slavery provision designed to thwart the heinous practice. It is critical to understand that America's founding document is not racist.

The pro-slavery interpretation of the three-fifths clause is simply the southern point of view. This argument holds that the founders were racists and is seemingly confirmed by the slave-owning Thomas Jefferson (the founder of the Democratic Party). The northern point of view is rarely, if ever, mentioned, nor is the fact that the founders included slavery opponents Samuel Adams, Stephen Hopkins, Benjamin Rush, Elbridge Gerry, James Wilson, John Adams, Roger Sherman, Benjamin Franklin, and John Witherspoon.

# The Building Blocks: Black Support for the GOP

In 1789, a year after the Constitution was ratified, Congress expanded its effort to end slavery by passing the Northwest Ordinance, which forbade slavery in federal territories and established how territories could become states. Essentially any new states would be free states. In 1808, Congress abolished the slave trade (though slavery was still practiced in the states). However, under a Democratic Congress, the Northwest Ordinance was reversed with the passage of the Missouri Compromise in 1820. With this new law, the Democratic Congress promoted slavery and permitted it in almost half of the federal territories.

The Democratic Congress passed other laws supporting slavery such as the Fugitive Slave Law of 1850 (requiring northerners to return escaped slaves to their masters and effectively sanctioning the kidnapping of freed slaves by slave hunters) and the Kansas-Nebraska Act of 1854 (expanding slavery westward into new parts of the territory where slavery was previously restricted including what is now Kansas, Nebraska, Colorado, Wyoming, Montana, Idaho, North and South Dakota).

With the onslaught of the pro-slavery agenda, anti-slavery Democrats in Congress joined with anti-slavery members from the Whigs, Free-Soilers, and emancipationists to fight slavery and secure civil rights for black Americans. That party they formed was called the Republican Party!

# Sumner v. Brooks

In 2009, in response to excessive federal spending under the Omnibus Stimulus Bill, the Troubled Asset Relief Program, and the bailouts of the automobile industry titans, a peaceful movement calling itself the Tea Party emerged from the electorate. Notwithstanding the wholly unfounded claims of racism within the movement, Tea Party rallies were without violence. However, Democratic activism has its roots in violence as far back as 1856.

In that year, Republican Senator Charles Sumner of Massachusetts, a champion of desegregating public schools in Boston and a promoter of civil rights, gave a two-day speech in the Senate against slavery. Following his speech, Democratic Representative Preston Brooks of South Carolina marched across the Rotunda from the House to the Senate; arriving on the Senate floor where Sumner was standing, he clubbed Sumner nearly to death, to the delight of many Democrats.

After three-and-a-half years of recovery, Sumner returned to the Senate. His first speech was against slavery. He was a hero of the anti-slavery movement—a Republican.

The Republican Party was soon to make a difference in the lives of black Americans.

The new party launched its first presidential bid in 1856. A northern phenomenon, the party ran John C. Fremont against James Buchanan. The Republicans promoted equality and civil rights for blacks while the Democrats promoted fear that ending slavery would be dangerous and ruin the happiness of the people.[5] The Republicans lost the election.

In 1860, the Republicans launched their second presidential bid. They ran Abraham Lincoln against US Senator Stephen Douglas, an Illinois Democrat. The party's platform was similar to its platform in 1856. Republicans blasted the Fugitive Slave law and added their opposition to the Supreme Court's *Dred Scott* decision; they were intent on ending slavery. The *Dred Scott* decision declared that blacks were not persons or citizens but were property with no rights. The decision was the single greatest aid to the pro-slavery movement at the time and provided a stark contrast between the Democrats, who supported it, and the Republicans, who did not.

Buchanan supported the Fugitive Slave Law and the *Dred Scott* decision. The ruling upheld the notion that some human life was not valuable. This thought is prevalent even today in the struggle over saving the innocent lives of unborn babies, with nearly 80 percent of Democrats rabidly supporting the pro-choice position. The "disposable-property ideology"[6] is a century-and-a-half old, and blacks continue to feel its effects in the abortion industry: they make up 13 percent of the population but account for 40.2 percent of abortions. In fact, for every hundred live births for blacks, there are fifty-three aborted black babies.

In 1860, there was a split in the party between the northern and southern Democrats, and so the northerner Stephen Douglas wasn't the only Democrat running. The northern Democrats supported slavery but did not want the South to secede from the North to form its own nation, while the southern Democrats were willing to do so. The northern Democrats voted for Douglas, while the southern Democrats voted for John C. Breckinridge or John Bell of the Constitutional Union Party. This split gave Lincoln 40 percent of the popular vote but 59 percent of the Electoral College vote.[7]

Lincoln, the Republican, had won! The party also took the House and Senate, placing the power to undo slavery firmly in Republican hands.

While Lincoln opposed slavery, he was not one of the Radical Republicans, the liberals of the era who wanted to abolish slavery.

Lincoln made it clear that he had no intention of ending slavery where it existed but was firmly against secession by the South.

However, the South feared Lincoln's plans and so his victory had consequences, bringing the secession of South Carolina in 1861 followed by Mississippi, Florida, Alabama, Georgia, Louisiana, and Texas. Virginia, Arkansas, Tennessee, and North Carolina came next.

Southern Democrats left Congress and formed their own country—the Confederate States of America, a slaveholding nation,[8]under President Jefferson Davis. This new nation was built upon the notion that the Negro was not equal to the white man and that slavery was the slave's natural and moral condition.[9] White supremacy was the guiding principle for these Democrats. Their mantra was "states' rights," a code phrase used by slavery-minded southerners, who later employed the term to oppress blacks through black codes, segregation, and institutional racism.

The division over economic, political, social, and psychological issues was complex and primarily revolved around slavery and its expansion into the federal territories. These divisions led to the Civil War, also called the War of Secession or the War of Rebellion, fought between the Union Army of the North and the Confederate Army of the South, beginning in 1861.

President Lincoln, attempting to avoid hostilities with the South, signaled to South Carolina that supplies were being delivered to Fort Sumter. Fearing a trick, South Carolina demanded that Major Robert Anderson surrender the fort. When he refused, on April 12, 1861, the first shots rang out and the Civil War began.

While southern Democrats were intent on furthering slavery as the dominant industry in the South, Republicans handed the slaves their freedom. Lincoln, aware of the public's growing support for the abolition of slavery, signed the Emancipation Proclamation. It took effect on January 1, 1863, and all slaves in the South were considered free.

Republicans understood the Emancipation Proclamation was not enough. Frederick Douglass explained, "[We] have the [Emancipation] Proclamation of January 1863. It was a vast and glorious step in the right direction. But unhappily, excellent as that paper is—and much as it has accomplished temporarily—it settles nothing. It is still open to decision by courts, canons [agency interpretations], and Congress."[10]

Consequently, the 1864 Republican platform called for a constitutional amendment to abolish slavery. Lincoln was re-elected with Democrat Andrew Johnson as his vice president in November 1864, and Republicans began to systematically dismantle slavery.

The South was defeated shortly after the election. On April 9, 1865, Confederate General Robert E. Lee surrendered to Union General Ulysses S. Grant at the Appomattox courthouse in Virginia. Five days later, the Great Emancipator was assassinated. On April 14, 1865, Lincoln, while watching a performance of *Our American Cousin* at Ford's Theatre in Washington, D.C., was shot by John Wilkes Booth, who conspired with nine others to kill the president and avenge the Confederate defeat.

The Civil War resulted in 620,000 deaths but ultimately gave birth to freedom for more than three million slaves in the fifteen slaveholding states. Johnson's reconstruction plan provided a framework to admit the South back into the Union and offer amnesty to Confederate loyalists.

However, Johnson, who came from Tennessee, was closely aligned with and sympathetic to the South as evidenced by his veto of civil rights bills and the Trumbull Freedmen's Bureau during his presidency;[11] he also rescinded the order granting land to the freed slaves.[12] That's right: a Democrat took back the promise of forty acres and a mule. The Republican Congress ultimately forged ahead with two dozen civil rights bills, and the Freedmen's Bureau helped change the lives of the freed slaves.

In 1865, with no help from the president, the House passed the Thirteenth Amendment to abolish slavery. All eighty-six Republicans voted to end slavery, but only fifteen of the sixty-five Democrats did. A year earlier, all thirty Republicans voted for the amendment in the Senate, while just four of nine Democrats did.

It would stand to reason that blacks would always remain loyal to the Great Emancipator and his party for these reasons alone.

Because Republicans were the leading abolitionists, the freed slaves naturally gravitated toward the party. When they gained the right to vote, they voted 100 percent for the Republican ticket and did so for a long period, beginning in the Reconstruction Era. Most blacks are unaware of the journey they have taken as a group, from overwhelming support for the Republican Party to 95 percent[13] backing for the Democratic Party today. Key milestones along the way track the Republicans' loss of black support from Reconstruction to the present.

# Reconstruction: The Forgotten Legacy

The Reconstruction Era, lasting from 1865 to 1877, saw great political and social development among blacks in America. The goal was to reconstruct the South and US society as a whole. It was a milestone era that temporarily opened the doors of freedom and equality to former slaves but also was a time of great conflict. It was the product of the Civil War. The Radical Republicans, the liberals of the day, moved their agenda without the help of President Andrew Johnson.

The defeated South was overseen by 17,600 federal troops at the beginning of the era; the number was reduced to six thousand by 1876. The South felt like it was under occupation and greatly resented that, but blacks were protected and as such allowed to prosper in society. They were lawyers, doctors, businessmen, teachers, ministers, and the like. They experienced unprecedented accomplishment.

Within a year of the new Thirteenth Amendment, blacks were registering to vote and began to nibble on the first fruits of civil rights and form Republican parties all across the South, thanks to the protections afforded them.

Southerners, known by Republicans as rebels, were required to swear an oath of allegiance to the United States and to the civil rights of blacks. Many refused, and Republicans became the political majority in the South for a time.

Republican legislators moved quickly to protect the voting rights of blacks, to prohibit segregation, to establish education for them, and to open public transportation, schools, and other institutions to blacks.[14] By 1870, nine of the reconstructed states had black male voter registration rates of at least 85 percent, which opened the door for the election of blacks, all of whom were Republicans.[15]

In Texas, the first forty-two black representatives elected to state legislature were all Republicans. In Louisiana, the first ninety-five black representatives and the first thirty-two black senators elected to the legislature were Republicans. In Alabama, the first 103 blacks elected to the legislature were Republicans. In Mississippi, the first 112 blacks elected to the legislature were Republicans. In South Carolina, the first 190 blacks elected to the legislature were Republicans. In Virginia, the first forty-six blacks elected to the legislature were Republicans. In Florida and North Carolina, the first thirty blacks elected to the legislatures were Republicans. In Georgia, forty-one blacks were elected to the legislature as Republicans.[16]

In addition, the first twenty-two black members of Congress were elected during Reconstruction, all Republicans from the old Confederacy. Hiram Rhodes Revels of Mississippi became the first black United States Senator, a Republican.

The first black Democrat would not be elected to the House of Representatives until 1935. That member was Arthur W. Mitchell from Illinois, a northern state.[17]

Many of these elected officials were former slaves and included self-made businessmen, lawyers, ministers, teachers, college presidents, a banker, and a publisher.

Democrats did not take the progress of the Republican Party lying down. Recall the bludgeoning of Senator Sumner in 1856? When the Democrats of this era were losing, they resorted to violence.

In 1866, in response to the enormous gains of blacks and the Republican Party, Democrats, in conjunction with city police and the Democratic mayor, attacked the Republican convention in New Orleans, killing forty blacks and twenty whites and wounding 150 others.[18]

In 1875, Democrats rushed the floor of the Louisiana Legislature to seize power from the elected black Republicans. They failed when federal troops arrived to restore order.

Violence against Republicans became commonplace in state after state, and the often deadly attacks were led by the Ku Klux Klan, formed by Democrats to tear down the Republican establishment (whites and blacks alike) and to restore power to themselves. Correct: the KKK began not as a racist organization per se but as a political tool against Republicans.[19]

Blacks were terrorized by murder and public flogging and were given a reprieve only if they vowed not to vote Republican. If they failed to get in line, the punishment was death.

These and other tactics tore away at the Thirteenth Amendment. Democrats found ways to circumvent the civil rights of the freed slaves by denying them citizenship in the states the party still controlled. Congress responded with the Fourteenth Amendment declaring that former slaves were full citizens of the states in which they lived and were thereby accorded all the rights and privileges of any other citizen in a state.

Not a single Democrat voted for the Fourteenth Amendment, while 94 percent of Republicans voted to pass the civil rights amendment.

Passage of the Fifteenth Amendment, the third postwar civil rights amendment, soon followed. The Fifteenth Amendment guaranteed blacks the right to vote. Like the Thirteenth and the Fourteenth Amendments, it was passed virtually by Republican votes alone.

From 1866 to 1875, Congress passed nearly two dozen civil rights bills, ranging from protecting the marriages of blacks to safeguarding voting rights and other civil rights. These bills were routinely vetoed by Democratic President Andrew Johnson but overridden by Republican legislators.

Massive voter intimidation persisted throughout the South as Democrats prevented blacks from voting for Republicans.

# The Election of 1876: The Great Compromise

The progress during Reconstruction was soon undone. Democrats and Republicans together struck a significant blow to blacks in the Great Compromise of 1877 agreeing to remove federal troops from the South and thus end protection for blacks.

The presidential election of 1876 was between Republican Rutherford B. Hayes and Democrat Samuel Tilden. Congress was divided, with Democrats controlling the House for the first time since before the Civil War. They were thus able to block all civil rights progress for blacks. Republicans no longer held full power and could not pass civil rights bills.

One-hundred-eighty-five electoral votes were needed to win the presidency. Tilden received 184 and Hayes 165. However, twenty disputed electoral votes had not yet been awarded.[20] The presidency could go either way.

The outstanding votes depended on the election numbers in Democratic districts where the black vote had been suppressed through intimidation. Picture an armed gunman waiting beside the ballot box to ensure that black voters reached the "right" decision. Few blacks turned out to vote. Recall the election of Barack Obama in 2008 and the voter intimidation case of *United States v. New Black Panther Party*. The images of Black Panthers armed with billy clubs at the entrance of a polling place come to mind. Recall the investigations of ACORN and its employees in fifteen states over allegations of voter fraud in the 2008 election and the felony conviction against the organization in Nevada in 2011.

In the election of 1876, it was discovered that the Democratic candidate for president had engaged in direct bribery of election officials in the disputed precincts.[21] Imagine that!

The Electoral College refused to count any disputed votes, and so the House of Representatives had to decide the election pursuant to the Twelfth Amendment. A deal had to be struck.

Congress impaneled a commission made up of seven Democrats and eight Republicans drawn from the House, the Senate, and the Supreme Court.

The commission determined that indeed there had been voter suppression through the killing, injuring, and intimidation of blacks by Democrats, and by a vote of 8-7 awarded the election to Republican Hayes.[22]

The House refused to ratify the commission's findings. There was a stalemate for four months. America had no president.

The solution, now called "The Great Compromise," was proposed by Democrats. To gain ratification of the commission's findings and deliver the presidency to the GOP, Republicans had to agree to withdraw federal troops from Florida, Louisiana, and South Carolina.

Republicans agreed and Reconstruction officially ended in the South. The South became known as the "solid Democratic South" and white supremacy was reestablished there. Hayes became president, but the political careers of all black Republican elected officials from the South ended. Blacks would not hold office in the South again for decades.[23]

The Great Compromise, along with the Democrats' systematic plan to reverse all civil rights measures, ended all progress for blacks. Control of the South fell into the hands of Democrats, and black codes and Jim Crow became the governing policies.

Blacks were prevented from traveling at certain hours and stopped from voting by literacy tests and poll taxes. Grandfather clauses stipulated that all men or lineal descendants of men who were voters before 1867 did not have to meet the educational, property, or tax requirements for voting. This effectively allowed all white males to vote while denying the voting right to black men. The grandfather clause became the centerpiece of a much larger system of discrimination and racial segregation.[24]

As Democrats regained control of the southern legislatures, state constitutions were rewritten to disenfranchise blacks. With these tactics, black voter registration plummeted and blacks were quickly voted out of federal and state offices. Within a single generation after

Reconstruction began, blacks were excluded from jury service, prohibited from marrying interracially, and subject to segregation in schools and in public accommodations. Without civil rights laws and protections, blacks lost the political and social development gained in the preceding twelve years provided by the Republicans. By 1911, Democrats had repealed 94 percent of Reconstruction legislation.[25]

# The Lily-White Movement

The end of Reconstruction in 1877 brought about a shift in the political landscape. Democrats successfully branded the Republican Party as the party of the Negro that wanted black domination of whites. The South was controlled by the Democrats, threatening the Republican Party on a national basis. Blacks migrated in large numbers to the North, presenting an opportunity for Republicans there but further diminishing the GOP footprint in the South.

To compete for voters, Republican leaders responded to the political shift by becoming more like Democrats in hopes of gaining control of southern governments. They softened their support for blacks and began to look more like the conservative Democrats of the day.

This shift split the Republican Party. The party divided into the "lily-whites" and the "blacks and tans,"[26] both vying for control of the GOP. By the end of the nineteenth century, the lily-whites had won the battle. They opposed black political participation and supported the return of segregation and white supremacy. They worked hand in hand with Democrats to drive blacks out of the political process.

Blacks and liberal whites, represented by "black and tan" parties from the 1880s to the 1960s, embraced Reconstruction-era policies. People in this segment of society had nowhere to go; they were not welcomed by the lily-whites or the Democrats. They were fighting for their survival with great hope that the Republican Party could be restored to its roots of equality and freedom.

They were met with violence from the lily-whites over party control as evidenced by a race riot in Texas in 1888 when white Republicans attempted to seize control from blacks at the GOP state convention.[27]

The lily-whites were supported by the national Republican establishment, and blacks and liberal whites were effectively disenfranchised from the political process.

The Republican effort to be seen as a conservative alternative to the long-established conservative Democrats failed. However, Republicans succeeded in alienating their historical base among blacks and were impotent throughout the South.[28]

The southern Democrats, firmly rooted in racism and a white supremacy agenda, wreaked havoc with blacks for the next ninety years.

# The New Deal

While southern Democrats furthered a white supremacy agenda, northern Democrats inched their way toward the black community created by the shifting demographics. While Republicans made futile efforts to attract more whites in the South by acting like conservative Democrats, northern Democrats, acting like liberal Republicans, made efforts to attract the blacks who had fled to the North to escape black codes and Jim Crow. The 1930s was a defining era for race politics.

The Great Depression began on the watch of Republican President Herbert Hoover, caused in part by the stock market crash of 1929 and multiple bank failures. Although Hoover lost to Franklin D. Roosevelt in the election of 1932, blacks were still loyal to the Republican Party and handed Hoover three-fourths of their vote despite FDR's solicitation of their support.[29] This loyalty continued well into the twentieth century.

This Depression disproportionately affected blacks. By 1931, one-third of southern urban blacks were jobless.[30] One year later, that figure grew to one-half. To make matters worse, jobs normally considered appropriate for the Negro, like janitorial and sanitation work, were now being given to whites. It became policy to fire blacks in favor of hiring whites for "Negro jobs."[31]

The collapse of the economy on Hoover's watch along with his weak plank on civil rights hurt black support for the party.

Roosevelt quickly filled the void. Although his New Deal was not designed to benefit blacks specifically but the larger white economy as a whole, Roosevelt drew blacks away from the Republican Party. His creation of the Fair Employment Practices Committee and the Works Progress Administration was credited with providing basic earnings for one million black families.[32] These moves created white-collar work for blacks and a small class of black bureaucrats.[33]

Under Secretary of the Interior Harold Ickes, segregation was ended in Interior Department cafés and restrooms in 1933; the Public Works Administration was required to hire skilled and unskilled black laborers; there were significant housing set-asides for blacks, and millions of dollars were spent repairing black schools, hospitals, and recreational facilities.[34]

Blacks had a rational response; they supported the New Deal administration and a new Democratic agenda that benefited them, albeit coincidentally.

Under Roosevelt, Democrats for the first time placed language in their platform calling for an end to racial discrimination.[35] Roosevelt by no means can be called an advocate for civil rights. He insulated himself from black leaders, refused to desegregate the armed forces, and had no staffers dedicated to racial issues. He was singularly focused on the national economy. Any benefit to the Negro was purely a byproduct of the success of his larger agenda. However, the new policies were beneficial to blacks in any event, and they became more sympathetic to Democrats. This would ultimately benefit the party.

It was not until Democrat Harry S. Truman became president that Democrats began vigorously advocating civil rights protections for blacks.

# Harry Truman and the Dixiecrats

Harry Truman's Committee on Civil Rights, formed in 1947, set the civil rights agenda for the next twenty years with a ten-point legislative package. It called for voting rights for blacks, equal employment opportunities, and legislation to prohibit racial violence (e.g., lynching), segregation, and poll taxes. This was the first plan of its kind since Reconstruction. Southern Democrats killed Truman's proposals, but he was able to desegregate the armed forces under Executive Order 9981.

Harry Truman's aggressive civil rights platform caused a problem among some Democrats who were not yet friendly to a civil rights movement within the party.

At the 1948 Democratic National Convention, in response to Truman's pro-civil rights platform, a group of protesting southern Democrats walked out to repudiate the move toward racial harmony that Truman sparked. They formed the States' Rights Democratic Party, later called the Dixiecrats.

*Marc T. Little*

The Dixiecrats mounted a campaign against Truman; they drafted South Carolina Governor J. Strom Thurmond as their presidential nominee, with "Segregation Forever" as their slogan, and almost cost Truman the election.

Truman's stand was a signal to blacks that a Democrat was willing to fight for their equality.

Major legislation was passed that guaranteed civil rights, voting rights, and fair housing for blacks. Truman's stand may have been the single most significant event leading blacks to the Democratic Party. Fifty-six percent of blacks shifted their party affiliation to the Democrats during this time.[36] Democrats now enjoyed support from the majority of black voters.

The 1948 election also signified the beginning of the end of the reign of the racist southern Democrats. These events caused many southern Democrats to leave the Democratic Party for the Republican Party. That was not helpful in attracting blacks to the GOP.

# The Civil Rights Act of 1964 and the Voting Rights Act of 1965

Make no mistake, history has given Democrats credit for passing the landmark civil rights legislation of the 1960s, and Democrat Lyndon B. Johnson specifically was a hero to black Americans. Because of this gift of credit, it is little known that but for Republican votes, Democrats could not have passed the bills. Johnson would not have been able to sign the civil rights legislation of 1964 and 1965 if Republicans in Congress had not cast their votes in support.

Johnson got 152 Democratic votes in the House and forty-six in the Senate for the Civil Rights Act, short of majorities in both houses; he got 138 Republican votes in the House and twenty-seven in the Senate, putting the legislation over the top. The Voting Rights Act passed in the House with 82 percent Republican support. The legislation would have failed in the Senate but for the thirty Republican votes.[37]

Republicans overwhelmingly supported the president. It stands to reason, since the heart of the bills came from Republican President Dwight D. Eisenhower, who preceded John F. Kennedy.

The disenfranchisement laws and policies created and enforced by southern Democratic legislatures were finally dead thanks to Lyndon Johnson and Republicans in Congress.

However, Republicans received no credit for the part they played in passing the landmark acts. In fact, it was rumored that if Republicans had gained the presidency or Congress, they would not have extended the Voting Rights Act and would have denied blacks the right to vote.[38] These misperceptions continue to drive a wedge between blacks and Republicans today.

# An Ideological Switch

The Radical Republicans, the force behind furthering the Reconstruction agenda, were known as liberals in the nineteenth century. Liberals, historically speaking, desire to change the status quo. They like to shake things up.

Southern Democrats, on the other hand, were the conservatives in the nineteenth century and continued to be so for another hundred years. Conservatives, historically speaking, cling to the status quo. They like things to stay just the way they are; generally speaking, change is not good in a conservative's eyes.

Radical Republicans wanted to end slavery at all costs; they wanted to change the status quo. Democrats, on the other hand, fought and lost their lives to keep slavery and even to expand it.

Following abolition, the political game could no longer be about slavery, and so it became more about power and control of the state governments and which party would lead the country.

In making that transition, many liberals and conservatives began reevaluating their party affiliations, since the political parties were now realigning their focuses based on racial realities in the North and South.

In fact, the Republican Party was formed by disaffected Americans jumping from one political party to another. Members of the American, Free Soil, and Whig parties, along with some northern Democrats, organized themselves under the new party name.

A wave of prominent southern Democrats with well-known racist agendas fled to the Republican Party after 1960. These defectors gave the Republican Party a bad name and drove a further wedge between Republicans and blacks. Some of the congressional Democrats switching parties were Floyd Spence (1962), Strom Thurmond (1964), Jesse Helms (1971), Trent Lott (1972), and Phil Gramm (1983).

While most believe that those with racist pasts joined the Republican Party so they would feel comfortable and at home in their ideological skin, few understand that party switching can and did occur for other reasons. Officials also switch parties to stand a better chance of reelection after legislative redistricting or to curry favor with the party in control to keep seniority and power in Congress.

Indeed, many defected to the Republican Party because Democrats began to embrace a liberal agenda that included civil rights for blacks while Republicans became the conservatives who slowly took control of the South and mostly aligned with the racial status quo. The GOP's Reconstruction roots were no longer visible; Republicans were busy attracting white conservative voters in the South and were no longer wearing the civil rights badge for which they were once known. Democrats looked far more attractive to blacks at this stage, and the party was nearly assured of a monopoly on black support.

# A Southern Strategy?

As if prominent racist Democrats joining the Republicans weren't enough to alienate black voters, Richard Nixon's so-called Southern Strategy delivered yet another blow to black support for Republicans— or so many historians would have us believe.

The "Southern Strategy" is said to be a scheme by Republicans to use race as a wedge issue to garner more white votes. We are told that GOP candidates would use buzz phrases like *states' rights* and *busing* to excite the white voter without care for the nonwhite voter. This tactic was supposedly first used by Barry Goldwater in 1964 and then made popular by Richard Nixon in the 1968 election.

This "strategy" was given credence particularly when Ken Mehlman, then the chairman of the Republican National Committee, appeared before the NAACP on July 14, 2005, and apologized for GOP tactics.

"By the '70s and into the '80s and '90s," he said, "the Democratic Party solidified its gains in the African American community, and we Republicans did not effectively reach out. Some Republicans gave up on winning the African American vote, looking the other way or trying to benefit politically from racial polarization. I am here today as the Republican chairman to tell you we were wrong."

Many have labeled opposition to abortion and same-sex marriage as "southernization," an extension of the strategy to drive a wedge and garner white support.

The reality is, any strategy that strengthens one party over the other will be met with criticism. In this case, Democrats have been successful at painting Republicans as racists. Most people who don't evaluate the claim believe the lie. Simple.

Bob Bostock, a former Nixon aide, wrote a compelling article titled "Debunking the Myth of the Nixon 'Southern Strategy.'" Written for the Nixon Library, it appeared on September 3, 2009. His take on the history of this president makes sense and is more credible than the tale of a conspiracy that allegedly spanned every Republican administration from Nixon to George W. Bush. Bostock writes,

> Over the years, however, [Richard Nixon's] critics have blamed him for creating a "Southern Strategy" designed to win white votes by exploiting racial tensions. If that had been his aim, the results of the 1968 election suggest he failed at it miserably. In 1968, RN lost four of the five Southern states that Goldwater had carried. George Wallace carried the rest of the Goldwater Southern bloc—Alabama, Georgia, Louisiana, and Mississippi. And of those four states, RN ran third, behind both Wallace and the Democrats' nominee, Hubert Humphrey, in three of them.

Once in the White House, President Nixon's actions can hardly be called those of a president seeking to inflame racial tensions. Nothing illustrates that better than the historic progress his administration achieved in finally ending the practice of segregating the races in "separate but equal" schools in the South. When RN took office in 1969, 68 percent of black Southern students attended segregated schools. Within five years, that number had been cut to 9 percent. As Tom Wicker wrote in his biography, *One of Us*, "The Nixon administration did more in 1970 to desegregate Southern school systems than had been done in the sixteen previous years, or probably since."

Of course, beginning in 1972, the Democrats' once Solid South turned reliably red at the presidential level, except when a Son of the South was running for president (Carter in 1976 and Clinton in 1992). The lock the Democrats had on southern Senate and House seats also began to erode during the Nixon years.

The reasons for this change are many. Chief among them is RN's success in occupying the middle ground in American politics and thus attracting the support of the Silent Majority, not just in the South, but also in every part of America. Attributing the Republican Party's success in breaking the Democrats' hold on the South to a cynical, Nixon-devised "Southern Strategy" based on creating and then exploiting racial division is not only simplistic, it's also contradicted by the record.

I tend to agree with Bostock. Unfortunately, just as many believe that Republicans had nothing to do with passing the civil rights legislation of 1964 and 1965, many also believe that Republicans used race strategically and negatively to garner white votes. This myth perpetuates Republican difficulty in garnering support from blacks.

For more than fifty years, Republicans have failed to understand how to reach out to black voters, but to believe there has been a conspiracy from one Republican administration to the next, using race to divide one group from the other, is to buy a curious myth based on speculation.

From Reconstruction to the civil rights movement of the '60s, Democrats ran the table on Republicans. Republicans let a monopoly of support from blacks diminish into less than 5 percent backing in 2008.

# Chapter 4:
## The Train from Washington Is One Hundred Years Overdue

*(During Reconstruction, freed slaves were promised forty acres and a mule. They were told that a man with their legal papers could be expected on a train from Washington. Some waited for him, and there are folks still waiting for him.)*

*But you can't depend on the train from Washington.*
*It's one hundred years overdue.*
—Gil Scott Heron

When I speak to young people about accomplishment, success, and the philosophical differences between Republicans and Democrats, I often share the story of two uncles that I learned during my childhood, though I use a bit of artistic license.

One uncle is rich and the other is not. The young listeners are typically of college age. I pose the question as it was posed to me.

Consider the rich uncle. He supports you and wants you to have a college education, so he pays for your application fees and tuition, he buys you that new car you like so much, and he pays your rent while you're in school. All you have to do is go to class and graduate.

Would you like that deal? I ask. The young people answer with a resounding yes, just as I once did.

Then I say, consider the other uncle. He supports you, too, and wants you to have a college education. But instead of paying for your application fees, your tuition, your car, and your apartment, he hires you at his car dealership so you can work over the summer and pay for the things you want. By working, you'll learn basic skills, acquire a work ethic, understand the need to show up on time to work, and appreciate the used car you can afford or the apartment in the part of town that fits your paycheck.

How about that deal? I ask. The young people are typically slouched down in their chairs by the time I get to the end of the metaphor. They always prefer the rich uncle.

Then I close the conversation with this: Let's say you took both deals and both uncles die in the middle of your education and you don't finish school. Which deal would you be better off with?

A light bulb goes on, and they get it. With one uncle, you were dependent; with the other uncle, you learned skills and became self-reliant.

Handouts hurt, robbing us of the opportunity to rely on ourselves to succeed. Hard work makes us all better; we appreciate those things we earn, and society is better for it.

Democratic presidents from Franklin D. Roosevelt to Barack Obama have told us that government is the answer to success and prosperity. Democrats believe it is the government's role to prop us up, to provide the tools we need, and then to sustain us. We can look back over time to determine how well that has worked. Roosevelt's New Deal was really a raw deal, the grandfather of out-of-control federal spending.

The chart below chronicles some of the federal spending on social programs from 1980 to 2010. Notice the amazing increase in spending in just thirty years.

| Began | Social Program | 1980 | 2010 | Increase/ Decrease |
|-------|----------------|------|------|--------------------|
| 1935 | Social Security | $270 billion | $590 billion | 119% Increase |
| 1944 | Education Assistance for Veterans | $6.4 billion | $9.7 billion | 50.9% Increase |
| 1946 | Child Nutrition | $9.35 billion | $17.3 billion | 85% Increase |
| 1956 | Disability Benefits | $39.7 billion | $124 billion | 213% Increase |
| 1964 | Permanent Food Stamp Program | $24.1 billion | $72.5 billion | 201% Increase |
| 1965 | Pell Grant Program | $13.5 billion | $45.3 billion | 237% Increase |
| 1965 | Medicare | $89.8 billion | $529 billion | 489% Increase |
| 1965 | Medicaid | $36.9 billion | $275 billion | 646% Increase |
| 1974 | SSI | $15.2 billion | $44 billion | 191% Increase |
| 1975 | Earned Income Tax Credit | $3.37 billion | $49.5 billion | 1370% Increase |
| 1975 | WIC | $1.9 0 billion | $7.70 billion | 306% Increase |

| 1981 | Energy Assistance | $4.17 billion | $4.99 billion | 19.7% Increase |
| 1996 | TANF | $18.3 billion | $22.5 billion | 22.7% Increase |
| 2010 | Health Care and Education Reconciliation Act and the Patient Protection and Affordable Care Act | Expands eligibility for Medicaid, provides subsidies to purchase health insurance, and expands Pell Grant Program.[1] | | |

Republicans believe that the uncle who wants to show you how to succeed with your own two hands, and not Uncle Sam, is more helpful in the long run.

The inability to appreciate the differences between these two philosophies plagues the black community.

My friend Johnny Griggs, a leading civil litigator in Los Angeles and a die-hard liberal Democrat, shares my enjoyment of a rich black cultural tradition—going to the neighborhood barbershop. Historically, blacks did not have the sort of private clubs where men could swap stories and share each other's company. Barbershops came to serve that purpose for working-class and professional blacks alike. The poor, middle-class, and rich black folks all got together in the barbershop—a cultural phenomenon.

You learn a great deal even today in those neighborhood gathering spots, and you also can tap into the prevalent mind-set. Johnny was getting his hair cut and his ears filled one day when the conversation turned to a frequent theme: the oppression of blacks and the lack of opportunities available to them.

One of the barbershop denizens was going on about the marginalization of black people, and he tried to reinforce his point by claiming that "Denzel Washington is one of the best acting brothers in Hollywood, and he has never gotten an Academy Award! That's proof the black man can't catch a break in this country!"

Johnny Griggs could no longer hold his tongue.

"I beg your pardon, but Denzel has not one but two Academy Awards—one for *Glory* and another for *Training Day*," he said.

The impassioned barber was not at all dissuaded by his patron's informed statement of fact.

"Oh no, he don't have any Academy Awards," he said flatly, before continuing his perpetual lament that blacks like him can't catch a break in the white man's America.

This is a terrible handicap. Many will not listen to or see reality all around them. Some in the black community are entrenched in victimhood. The challenge in the twenty-first century is to pry those fingers from such defeatism.

The mind-set of this friendly neighborhood barber is a snapshot of the victim mind-set of the entire black community. This mentality was created by the nanny state and proves the New Deal gravy train and its offspring were a raw deal and, in fact, failed by crippling, if not killing, the black family.

After the 1929 crash on Wall Street, unemployment rose as high as 25 percent, and families of all colors were out of work. Deporting Latinos and firing black men to fill positions with whites became the policy du jour. Instability, financially and psychologically, set in for all families. However, the black family was disproportionately affected by the New Deal.

Welfare was the cancer that destroyed the black family unit. Intended to deliver families from poverty into sustainable lifestyles, it fractured marriage, employment, health, and education. Only in 1996 did the United States begin to administer its brand of chemotherapy with welfare reform legislation.

In *"The 2010 Index on Government Dependence,"* William Beach and Patrick Tyrrell of the Heritage Foundation noted that in 1996, under President Bill Clinton, Congress passed the Welfare Reform Act, also known as the Personal Responsibility and Work Opportunity Reconciliation Act. This act replaced the Aid to Families with Dependent Children (AFDC) program—established in 1940 under Roosevelt during the Great Depression, entitling recipients to unconditional benefits—with Temporary Assistance for Needy Families (TANF), a block grant program. AFDC, an old cash welfare program, was intended to provide financial assistance to needy dependent children. Over the decades, however, the program swelled and added adults, such as unemployed, unmarried mothers of enrolled children. Welfare rolls peaked in 1994, reaching more than five million cases, or 14.2 million individual recipients.

An open-ended assistance program, AFDC handed out benefits without expectations. Recipients were entitled to cash aid as long as they fell below the need standards set by the states. The entitlement created perverse incentives—discouraging work among able-bodied adult recipients and discouraging marriage because a married woman with a child was ineligible.

"In 1960, welfare was so meager that only a small set of young women at the very bottom layer of society could think it was 'enough' to enable a woman to keep a baby without a husband," writes Charles Murray in the July 1992 issue of *Commentary*. "By 1970, it was 'enough,' both in the resources it provided and in the easier terms under which it could be obtained, to enable a broad stratum of low-income women to keep a baby without a husband. That remains true today."

"The welfare system, though intended as a 'compassionate safety net,' consumed $3 trillion in 25 years and trapped many in an endless cycle of poverty that does not reward individual initiative,"[2] said President George W. Bush.

"Before the welfare state," wrote research analyst Vedran Vuk, "there existed incentives to have children and insure your own future. Now, we have incentives to break the family apart. TANF actually gives more money to single moms. This may seem like a great program to help single mothers in need, but in reality, the program makes it easier for the man in the family to leave. It reduces the man's practical responsibility to stay and raise the child. The program creates more single mothers!"[3]

Beach and Tyrrell noted that welfare reform effectively altered the fundamental premise of receiving public aid and ended it as an entitlement. Assistance became temporary and was tied to demonstrable efforts by recipients to find work or take part in work-related activities. The self-sufficiency of recipients became the focus. The successes of welfare reform are undeniable. From August 1996 to September 2009, welfare caseloads declined by 57.5 percent, from 4.4 million families to 1.9 million families. The legislation also reduced child poverty by 1.6 million children.

The system of handouts—as recent as the Economic Opportunity Act, or War on Poverty, under President Johnson—disproportionately affected blacks. When the War on Poverty began in the 1960s, 7 percent of US children were born outside of marriage. Today, the number is 38 percent. Among blacks, it is 69 percent. The black family is in ruins today because of the War on Poverty and long-term government aid.

The share of black households headed by women grew from 28 percent to 40 percent from 1970 to 1980. The War on Poverty virtually threw black men out of their own homes. Is it any wonder there is a victim mentality in the black community? As a man, how can you fight Uncle Sam bringing home a paycheck?

Author Michael Fumento writes,

At the beginning of World War II, the illegitimate birth rate among black Americans was slightly less than 19%. Between 1955 and 1965—the year of the Watts riots and also the start of the War on Poverty—it rose slowly, from 22% to 28%. But beginning in the late 1960s the slow trend rapidly accelerated, reaching 49% in 1975 and 65% in 1989.

Empirical studies have borne out the theory that welfare is behind much of this disintegration.

For example, a study at the University of Washington showed that an increase of roughly $200 a month in welfare benefits per family correlated with a 150% increase in the illegitimate birth rate among teens.

According to the House Ways and Means Committee "Green Book" for 1990, about 40% of parents collecting AFDC were black, 38% white and 17% Hispanic. At that time, blacks accounted for about 12% of the population, while Hispanics were 9% of the population.[4]

A great deal of criticism can be leveled at the welfare state that began with the New Deal under Roosevelt, increased under Johnson's Great Society, and was amended in the '90s under Clinton. While welfare destroyed the black community, the New Deal at least created the Civilian Conservation Corps, a public works program that operated from 1933 to 1942, providing jobs for unemployed, unmarried men, ages eighteen to twenty-five, from families drawing relief. Blacks benefited from programs like these.

Reversing the adverse impact of decades of government dependence is critical for the survival of the black family. It means no longer seeking ongoing financial aid from the government; it means applauding your successes, but also blaming yourself, and no one else, for your failures; and it means recognizing that the Academy Award records are accurate— yes, Denzel has two Oscars! Finally, it means no longer waiting for the train from Washington. It didn't come then, and it ain't coming now.

The black community has to do a few simple things:

## 1. Value Marriage

The Census Bureau reports that children living at home with both parents grow up with more financial and educational advantages than those raised by one parent.[5]

In *The Audacity of Hope,* Barack Obama wrote,

> [C]hildren living with single mothers are five times more likely to be poor than children in two-parent households. Children in single-parent homes are also more likely to drop out of school and become teen parents, even when income is factored out. And the evidence suggests that on average, children who live with their biological mother and father do better than those who live in stepfamilies or with cohabiting partners ... In light of these facts, policies that strengthen marriage for those who choose it and that discourage unintended births outside of marriage are sensible goals to pursue.

Compared with similar children raised by two married biological parents, children raised in single-parent homes are more likely to fail in school, abuse drugs or alcohol, commit crimes, become pregnant as teens, and suffer from emotional and behavioral problems. Such children are also more likely to end up on welfare or in jail when they become adults.[6] We can reverse this trend.

If we value each other as men and women and take responsibility for the children we make together by honoring them with married parents, that alone would change our communities. The answer must no longer be aborting unwanted babies, or leaving them with nana, or walking out on the girl you thought was so fine until you heard the words "I'm pregnant."

We must value the institution of marriage and all that God intended it to be for the family and for the community at large, a force for good in society.

When we begin to raise children in two-parent households, the next generation will have more financial and educational advantages, as the statistics demonstrate, and we will then begin to break the cycle of government dependence. This will not change the community overnight, nor will it end the general relief check right away, but it is a seed that will grow into a tree tomorrow and change our grandchildren's destiny.

## 2. Value Education

We no longer use the old adage that said, "The one thing they can't take from you is your education." We have left that old truth on the sidelines of life's pursuits. Now, many of our children barely finish high school, with the dropout rate for blacks twice that of white students.[7]

The Supreme Court desegregated schools in 1954 with *Brown v. Board of Education* and paved the way for blacks to receive equal education. The battle to accomplish this cost the lives and hard work of civil rights activists over a long period. The price they paid has been squandered, and we don't seem to care.

One hundred Democrats in Congress issued the "Southern Manifesto," denouncing the court's decision to end segregation. They declared that desegregation was "certain to destroy the system of public education." [8]

Whites quickly opened private institutions far out of reach of blacks, and quality education just as quickly moved with them. "Separate but equal" was always a lie, but desegregation failed to bridge the educational divide after *Brown*. Public schools, particularly in the South, fell into disrepair and did not receive adequate instructors. And of course, public education is failing our students miserably now.

Perhaps the Democrats were right— the system is destroyed. But they destroyed it!

It is a crime that local and national teachers unions are fighting for higher wages while passing our kids from grade to grade though most cannot read or do math at grade level.

Democrats bent over backward prior to the decision in *Brown v. Board of Education* to keep blacks out of schools whites attended. Now that blacks are in those very schools, Democrats fight to keep them trapped there by denying meaningful voucher programs that would allow students to transfer to better schools. The left argues dismissively that voucher programs would simply be used to fund religious education.

This is a fight that Republicans have long waged on behalf of all students trapped in poor-performing schools. Republicans have fought for many years to benefit blacks who are disproportionately trapped in these schools. Why won't Democrats let them out? The answer: unions.

Until the states agree to take on the teachers unions, which generally are working for self-gain, and not for the students, or until vouchers can be widely implemented, the answer is parent engagement. We have to find time between busy work schedules, appointments, and the hustle and bustle of day-to-day life to focus on the educational pursuits of our kids. Are they showing up for school every day, or are they going in and leaving after we drop them off? Are they doing homework and bringing it in? What grades are they getting on their quizzes and final exams? Do they participate in classroom discussions? Are they well behaved in the classroom? Do we know?

Show up one day and sit in the classroom. Does your kid have on the same clothes he or she was wearing this morning? Is the teacher reading a newspaper or teaching the class? What's the principal's name? Do you know it?

Parent engagement is a must. My father taught me one thing in particular that I have never forgotten. He said, "Son, people do what you inspect, not what you expect."

We should have a reasonable assurance that the school and the teacher are qualified to teach. However, we should not expect teachers to give our kids the time and attention they need to value their education and do well—we should inspect to see that in fact they are doing so.

We must stem the tide of high school dropouts by reinforcing not only the importance of graduating from high school but the importance of going to college.

In 2010, as a founding board member, I had the privilege of opening Crown Preparatory Academy, a public charter school in Los Angeles, in response to the educational problems we face in that city. We are providing a rigorous and disciplined academic environment for fifth- through eighth-graders each day.

When we opened our doors to begin recruiting students, I was amazed at how many black parents refused to enroll their children because they didn't want them to wear a uniform or thought the homework demands were too great.

Our children do not value education today because their parents do not value it.

If we don't get this right, blacks will not be able to compete for jobs in the next generation and will be resigned to the "Negro jobs" of the 1930s—janitorial and sanitation. By then, turning the tide will take another generation.

### 3. Value hard work

Blacks have a history of being hard workers. Whether in the food service or hospitality industries, public finance, as doctors, lawyers, elected officials, teachers, entrepreneurs, entertainers or athletes, blacks excel in every segment of society. But the current generation did not inherit the work ethic of the previous generations.

Today, many, not all—I repeat, not all—black employees often drag into the workplace late. It's called CP (colored people's) time. They behave as if the employer is doing them a favor by employing them. I am a witness! They are often riding on the edge. If they're not late, they are one minute from being late. This is an everyday occurrence. It's a chronic issue in the black community. I, too, struggle to value my time and that of other's.

When some blacks are asked to do an assignment, God forbid if it seems slightly outside of the job description. They are often hostile to being team players and doing work beyond their perception of what the job calls for.

Unfortunately, the behavior of young black employees is often juxtaposed against the behavior of Hispanics, who, more often than not, are on time, if not early, and eager to work. If they finish an assignment, they often want to know what else they can do or they just do it without asking. (I've been told that my experience is fortunate and that there are convincing examples that Latino workers have many faults. too.)

Finally, when it comes time for a promotion, the on-time, team player gets the nod, I assure you.

The work ethic is a key to advancement, but first you must value the work. If you'd rather stay at home and collect a check from Uncle Sam, you will resent the workplace. Therefore, you must understand the value of work. As the old saying goes, "You are what you do."

Work traditionally provides a personal identity. An identity gives a person self-esteem and purpose. If you do nothing, it is nearly impossible to value yourself. With work, you develop self-esteem and an identity. With identity, self-esteem, and purpose, you can value yourself. You are important and valuable in your own mind. If you can value yourself, you will then value the work of your hands. When you value the work of your hands, you will take pride in all that you do. That pride will permeate your life in general, but most important, you will develop a work ethic. That's important.

Government dependence can be helpful for very short and defined emergencies, but long-term subsidy has been proven to destroy the black family. When welfare becomes a way of life, the person collecting the check has given up; there is no hope. Blacks must value marriage, education, and hard work as a means of breaking a seventy-year habit of taking from the (once) rich Uncle Sam, who is now robbing from Peter to pay Paul.

# Chapter 5:
## The Pied Pipers

*A leader takes people where they want to go ... a great leader takes
people where they don't necessarily want to go, but ought to be.*
——Rosalynn Carter

The Scriptures teach us that where there is no vision, the people perish. (Prov. 29:18) Vision comes from inspired leadership. The black community has been without inspired leadership for a very long time. In fact, the black community has been led astray while it generally ignores the real black heroes and heroines of our time like Honorable Condoleezza Rice, former national security adviser and secretary of state, and Supreme Court Justice Clarence Thomas.

The black community would rather follow unproven strangers or the loudest mouth offering something for free. As the villagers of Hamelin know, nothing is free.

Legend says that a mysterious man appeared in Hamelin, wearing a coat of many bright colors. He claimed to be a rat catcher. He promised that for a certain sum, he would rid the town of mice and rats. He struck a deal for a certain price with the townsmen to perform his service.

The rat catcher, called the Pied Piper, took a fife from his pocket and began to play it. As he played, mice and rats came from every house and gathered around him. He led them all into the River Weser. They followed him and drowned.

The townsmen marveled at his work but soon regretted the price they had agreed upon; they refused to pay, and the Pied Piper left angry and bitter.

He returned on June 26, early in the morning, with a dreadful look on his face and wearing a strange red hat. He took his fife from his pocket and began to play it; this time, all of the children in the town, four years old and up, 130 in all, followed the sound of the Pied Piper, who led them into a mountain cave. They disappeared, never to be seen again.

The townsmen had so angered him that his revenge was the death of their children and the town's very future.

Here is the problem with the story: where were all the mothers and fathers when the children were awakened early in the morning and led into the street to their deaths? Were they asleep? Were they in the fields? Where were they? The author of the story doesn't tell us, but we do know they didn't prevent the children from going astray. They were absent! They came looking for their children when it was too late.

Some blame politicians for the failures in the black community. For sure there is blame to be placed when career politicians have had scarce success in creating policies that address poverty, homelessness, failed schools, teen pregnancy, incarceration, and mortality in the communities they serve. But highlighting the failings of elected officials has proven to be a waste of time. We rarely unelect them. True leadership starts in the home. A few historical figures illustrate effective leadership traits we must aspire to have.

### 1.  Leadership is Compassionate.

Consider the Joseph of Genesis. Joseph, the beloved son of Jacob, was despised by his brothers because he was his father's favorite son. When his brothers got the chance, they sold Joseph into slavery. Joseph spent years and years as a slave working in Potiphar's house. He was gone for so long that his father thought he was dead.

Over time, God's favor shone on Joseph, who ultimately was elevated to a position of great trust in the house of the king of Egypt. In fact, Joseph was so esteemed that the king gave him dominion over all the food and livestock of Egypt.

A famine gripped Canaan, where Joseph's family lived, and all of Egypt, and Joseph's brothers came to Egypt begging for food.

Joseph's brothers stood before him, without recognizing him, pleading for food to take back to their ailing father. Joseph could have exacted punishment on his dreadful brothers. He could have tricked them into bringing his father to him and then killed them. He could have done a lot of things to take revenge. Instead, he sent them back with more food than they could carry. Ultimately, he revealed his identity, saw his father on his deathbed, and reunited the family.

Joseph was a leader. He was a leader not only with governmental authority to jail or kill his enemies, but a leader who had a compassionate heart.

Leadership looks beyond what is lawful to do and demonstrates compassion.

### 2.  Leadership Makes a Difference.

Steve Jobs was just a man with an idea, but his idea changed the world. Jobs was the founder of Apple; may he rest in peace. A memorial piece on *Entrepreneur.com* offers these thoughts:

Steve Jobs' vision of a "computer for the rest of us" sparked the PC revolution and made Apple an icon of American business. But somewhere along the way, Jobs' vision got clouded (some say by his ego), and he was ousted from the company he helped found. Few will disagree that Jobs did indeed impede Apple's growth, yet without him the company lost its sense of direction and pioneering spirit. After nearly 10 years of plummeting sales, Apple turned to its visionary founder for help, and a little older, a little wiser Jobs engineered one of the most amazing turnarounds of the 20th century.

The adopted son of a Mountain View, California, machinist [yes, his mother refused to abort him and had the wisdom to place him for adoption] … Jobs once described himself as a "hopeless romantic" who just wanted to make a difference. Quite appropriately like the archetypal romantic hero who reaches for greatness but fails, only to find wisdom and maturity in exile, an older, wiser Steve Jobs returned triumphant to save his kingdom.[1]

When you buy an iPhone, a Mac computer, an iPod, or any other Apple product, it comes with virtually nothing other than the product itself. You plug it in and it's simple to operate. When you look at an Apple product, your visual experience is simple. There is no clutter, no confusion—simplicity at its finest. It's intuitive. Similarly, the Apple website is without clutter and is user-friendly.

Steve Jobs had an idea that changed how the world communicates. Innovating the technology was certainly the reason for Apple's success, but he set a new standard for technology. The standard was simplicity.

### 3.  Leadership Requires Followers.

If you sent out a press release to your local newspaper announcing that you were appearing in the town square on Sunday at 2 p.m. for an important talk, would anyone show up? If you sent out an inter-office memorandum calling a meeting of your peers, would they come? If you sent out invitations to your neighbors to meet at your home to discuss your public school or community, how many would be interested? If you called a family meeting in your backyard on Saturday night, would your spouse and teenager be there, and if so, would they be interested in listening to what you have to say?

Leadership by definition requires followers; most effective leadership is wrapped with character. If you have a depth of character, others will respect you. (Character is doing what you say you will do; character is doing what you mean and meaning what you say.) When you have respect, others will trust you. If they trust you, they will follow you.

When you speak, do others listen? Do you even have something to say? If no one is following you, you are not leading; you're just on a stroll.

A National Park Service history tells us,

The Selma-to-Montgomery March for voting rights ended three weeks—and three events—that represented the political and emotional peak of the modern civil rights movement. On "Bloody Sunday," March 7, 1965, some 600 civil rights marchers headed east out of Selma on U.S. Route 80. They got only as far as the Edmund Pettus Bridge six blocks away, where state and local lawmen attacked them with billy clubs and tear gas and drove them back into Selma. Two days later on March 9, Martin Luther King, Jr., led a "symbolic" march to the bridge. Then civil rights leaders sought court protection for a third, full-scale march from Selma to the state capitol in Montgomery …

On Sunday, March 21, about 3,200 marchers set out for Montgomery, walking 12 miles a day and sleeping in fields. By the time they reached the capitol on Thursday, March 25, they were 25,000-strong. Less than five months after the last of the three marches, President Lyndon Johnson signed the Voting Rights Act of 1965—the best possible redress of grievances.[2]

Martin Luther King, Jr. led thousands in marches for freedom. Thousands followed him. He was a man of great character, a man who didn't mind calling a boycott, a man who didn't mind calling a meeting. He was a man who had something to say, and all listened.

### 4. Leadership is Visionary.

A leader sees the needs of tomorrow today. Whether the need is on the job, in your personal life, or in the lives of your spouse and children, you must anticipate the needs of tomorrow and get busy to prepare for that moment if you are to be a good leader. Visionary leadership is not always easy.

In its October 10, 2008 issue, *Entrepreneur* magazine tells this story:

Many of the 20th century's most influential entrepreneurs overcame tremendous odds in their quests for success. But none faced greater obstacles than Madam C. J. Walker. The daughter of former slaves, she was orphaned at the age of 7, married at 14, a mother at 17, and a widow at 20. Yet she was determined to build a better life for herself and her daughter. Starting with a meager investment of only $1.50, she built one of the most successful black-owned businesses of the early 20th century and became the nation's first woman self-made millionaire.

Walker was born Sarah Breedlove on December 23, 1867. Her parents were sharecroppers on the sprawling Burney cotton plantation in Delta, Louisiana, and like most children of her time, Sarah went to work in the cotton fields at an early age. After her parents died during a severe outbreak of yellow fever, Sarah moved to Vicksburg, Mississippi, to live with her sister, Louvenia. But the arrangement proved to be less than ideal. According to Sarah, Louvenia's husband was "a cruel and contemptuous scoundrel" who treated her terribly. To escape his tyranny, Sarah married a Vicksburg laborer named Moses McWilliams when she was only 14.

On June 6, 1885, Sarah gave birth to a daughter named Lelia. She believed that if she worked hard enough, she could provide her daughter with a better life than she had. Tragically, shortly after Lelia's second birthday, Moses was killed in an accident. At age 20, now a widow and a single mother, Sarah moved to St. Louis, where she worked as a laundress for $1.50 per day for the next 18 years. Working up to 14 hours per day, she scrimped and saved until she had enough money to send Lelia to Knoxville College.

By the time she was in her late 30s, Sarah's hair had started falling out due to a combination of stress and years of using damaging hair-care products. She was not alone. In fact, most black women of the time experienced the same problem but there were no hair-care products on the market to correct it. She tried everything that was available, but met with little success, so she started experimenting with her own hair-care products.

Her big break came in 1905, when, as she would later tell a reporter, "I had a dream, and in that dream a big black man appeared to me and told me what to mix up for my hair. Some of the remedy was grown in Africa, but I sent for it, mixed it, put it on my scalp, and in a few weeks my hair was coming in faster than it had ever fallen out. I tried it on my friends; it helped them. I made up my mind I would begin to sell it."

Starting with a few dollars' worth of chemicals, Sarah mixed batches of her products in her washtub and began selling them door to door to friends and neighbors. A natural marketer, Sarah pushed her products by giving free demonstrations. This technique worked and black women throughout St. Louis began buying her wares with enthusiasm. It was about this time that Sarah received word that her brother had died, leaving a widow and four daughters in Denver. She decided to move to Denver to help out. There, she continued selling her products door to door with tremendous success.

Shortly after she arrived in Denver, Sarah married newspaperman C. J. Walker and adopted Madam C. J. Walker as her professional name. With help from her husband, she began running advertisements in black newspapers and quickly developed a thriving mail- order business. After graduating from college, Lelia moved to Denver to help with the family venture, and before long, the Walkers were bringing in $10 per week—which was quite a lot of money at that time. C.

J. decided that the business had reached its full potential. His wife disagreed. She believed that black women across the country would be interested in her products, if only they knew about them. Leaving Lelia in charge of the mail-order business, Walker embarked on an extended sales tour throughout the southern United States. Within a few months, she was making weekly sales of $35—more than twice the salary of the average white American male worker and 20 times that of the average black woman worker.

Realizing that she could only do so much selling herself, Walker recruited and trained a team of door-to-door saleswomen to demonstrate and take orders for her products—much like Avon and Mary Kay Cosmetics would do decades later. With a team of trained saleswomen crisscrossing the country, Walker's company grew rapidly. In 1908, she expanded into the East, establishing a business office in Pittsburgh. Two years later, she built a large manufacturing plant in Indianapolis that would eventually employ more than 3,000 people.

By 1917, the Madam C. J. Walker Manufacturing Co. had become black America's most successful business and Madam C. J. Walker, America's first self-made woman millionaire. To celebrate her success, she commissioned black architect Vertner Tandy to design and build a lavish mansion for her on the Hudson River in Irvington, New York. Sadly, she was unable to enjoy her new home for long. For several years, Walker had been experiencing problems with high blood pressure. Her doctors advised her to take it easy, but Walker could not—or would not—slow down her hectic pace. Long years of traveling and hard work finally took their toll. On May 25, 1919, Walker died of kidney failure resulting from hypertension.

A woman of extraordinary courage and vision, Madam C. J. Walker blazed the trail for the generations of women entrepreneurs that would follow her. The grit and determination that carried her from a cotton field to a mansion, from abject poverty to riches, remain a burning inspiration for Americans of all races who yearn to realize their dream of achieving a better life.[3]

## 5. Leadership Embraces Responsibility.

On September 11, 2001, the terror attacks on the World Trade Center and the Pentagon changed America, if not the world, forever. Leading up to these attacks, both the Clinton and Bush administrations believed that Saddam Hussein had weapons of mass destruction. It was also widely understood that the terror plots against the United States were launched from Afghanistan from where al-Qaeda took responsibility for the events.

On October 7, 2001, President George W. Bush took responsibility for protecting the lives of American citizens by opening the war on terror against the Taliban and al-Qaeda forces in Afghanistan. Osama bin Laden was among the most valuable targets of this war.

As an extension of the war on terror, Bush launched Operation Iraqi Freedom on March 20, 2003, and toppled the murderous regime of Saddam Hussein to eliminate his weapons of mass destruction.

Hussein was captured hiding in a spider hole on December 13, 2003, and was hanged by his own people on December 30, 2006; the Iraqi people were given the gift of democracy, and America and its allies are rebuilding that nation, the only Arab democracy friendly to US interests in the region. Weapons of mass destruction were never found, and Bush's reliance on the intelligence that supported the invasion continues to plague the former president's legacy.

Bush's leadership after 9/11 was supported by Congress in an overwhelming show of solidarity. On October 11, 2002, Congress gave Bush the authority to take the nation to war in Iraq. The Senate voted 77–23; the House voted 296–133.[4]

As of June 2012, there had been 4,486 US fatalities in Operation Iraqi Freedom and 2,023 in Operation Enduring Freedom/Afghanistan.

The toll of the wars in Iraq and Afghanistan on America's military has been staggering as those men and women delivered liberty to the Middle East.

Whether or not you agree with the decision the president made to go into Afghanistan and then to Iraq, Bush did what many leaders fail to do—he accepted responsibility and then made a decision. He accepted the responsibility of the office of president, which, in part, is to protect the citizens of the United States. After 9/11, there were no more terrorist attacks on American soil during his administration.

### 6.  Leadership Can Be Revolutionary.

One leader can change a whole nation or even the whole world. I have had the opportunity to travel to South Africa more than fifteen times in the last ten years. South Africa is remarkable for so many reasons but particularly because of its journey from apartheid to an open democracy for all races. My first trip was in 2001 just a decade after the dismantling of the apartheid system.

Apartheid was a system of legal racial segregation very similar to Jim Crow in the South after Reconstruction. Black Africans essentially had no rights. Nonwhites were deprived of citizenship. They had no voting rights and no right to hold political office. They were confined to certain parts of the nation, their travel was heavily restricted, and they often came up missing.

The government segregated education, medical care, beaches, and other public accommodations, and provided black people with services inferior to those for white people. The system, enforced by the National Party government, maintained white control over all nonwhites. Well documented in Hollywood films, such as *Cry Freedom,* starring Denzel Washington as activist Steven Biko, and *Mandela and de Klerk,* starring Sidney Poitier, apartheid was a murderous system that began in the colonial era but was officially enacted in 1948. It spanned a generation until the 1990s with the help of many nations and businesses, including US firms.

As unrest spread and became more violent, state organizations responded with increasing repression and state-sponsored violence. But in 1990, under President Frederik Willem de Klerk, the apartheid system was dismantled. After multiracial democratic elections in 1994, the African National Congress emerged as the ruling political party, and black African Nelson Mandela, a political prisoner under apartheid, became president of the Republic of South Africa. Mandela, an ordinary man who became a hero for a nation, is one person who changed the world.

Mandela was an anti-apartheid activist and the leader of Umkhonto we Sizwe, the armed wing of the African National Congress.[5] In 1962, he was arrested and convicted of sabotage and other charges, and sentenced to life in prison. Mandela served twenty-seven years, spending much of that time on Robben Island before his release on February 11, 1990, which came after years of sanctions against the South African government and internal protest by the people.

*Madiba,* meaning *father* in his Xhosa native tongue, led the negotiations for his party with de Klerk and later led the entire country toward healing with an emphasis on reconciliation.

I have often marveled at the people in South Africa, black and white. It is as if some divine wand was waved over the nation to make healing possible. When you visit the shopping squares, you will see blacks and whites shopping together, eating together, and even dating one another. While the vestiges of apartheid are far from gone (blacks make up the majority of domestic workers, and the country's wealth is still largely in the hands of government-owned business or wealthy whites), the change is nonetheless miraculous.

I attended the Lenox Lewis-Hasim Rahman fight in South Africa on April 22, 2001. Rahman delivered a powerful right cross that knocked the champion to the mat. It was the shot heard round the world.

The next day, a meet-and-greet between Madiba and Lewis was scheduled to occur at the home of the president. I was the guest of Golden Gloves, the promoter of the fight, and was happy to attend.

I stood on the front porch and shook the hand of a legend; Nelson Mandela was and is a true revolutionary leader. He was a lawyer, a community activist who paid a price for his activism, stood up for his convictions, and was used by God to change a nation.

None of these examples of leadership involves saints or gods, only ordinary men and women who were born into unexceptional lives and made mistakes along the way but did extraordinary things because they had compassion and vision, accepted responsibility, and knew how to set a standard. Because of these things, others followed them and they all became revolutionary leaders.

We can be great leaders in our everyday lives by exhibiting the qualities of the leaders in our communities or wherever we can find them. The lives of our children, and the generations to come, depend on it.

When mothers and fathers lead, children will follow. That's what they do. Children grow and mature through imitation. They follow our examples and listen to the messages, verbal and nonverbal, that we give them. If the message is that going to school is not important, guess what? They won't go to school, they won't graduate, and they won't get jobs. And then what? If the message is that sex before marriage is "no big deal," guess what? They will have sex at an early age, they will get pregnant, they will drop out of school, they won't graduate, and they won't get jobs. And then what? What message are you sending your children or the children in your community? When they see you, do they aspire to be like you?

I often find myself contemplating my own legacy. What will I leave behind for the next generation? Will I make good use of the time God has given me, and what will be the evidence of that? These questions weigh on me as I strive to achieve what I believe are good goals in this lifetime and to leave an inheritance for my children's children.

I recently attended an event at my alma mater, the University of Southern California. I've seen no better example of leaving a legacy than the life of the late Sol Price, the son of Jewish immigrants and the founder of the Price Club. The Price Charities made a $50 million gift to the USC School of Public Policy Planning and Development. Consequently, the school is now called the USC Price School of Public Policy. It will perpetually assist students and communities around the nation in the areas of urban planning, public policy, real estate development, public administration, and health policy and administration.

I was honored to be invited to attend the luncheon after the donation ceremony; we gathered on the lawn in a tent directly in front of the Mark's International Hall dormitory where I spent my freshman year. I imagined that freshman, Marc Little, looking out of his window and onto the lawn below and scanning the attendees at the luncheon. In my mind's eye, I pictured that freshman fixated on himself, nearly thirty years in the future, and I wondered what he would say. Would he see something inspiring? Would he want to talk to "that guy"? Would he want to be like him? Would he see the evidence of a life well lived?

I suppose the answer to my questions will come in time. For now, I simply try to be the best husband, the best mentor, the best brother or son I can be. Time will have to take care of the rest.

When we wake up and find that the next generation has not improved from the current one, we cannot blame the Pied Piper. We must blame ourselves if we leave no inheritance. It is our choice to be absent, like the parents who let their children be led to their deaths by the Pied Piper, or to be present to ensure their lives, their livelihoods, and yes, even their success.

President George H. W. Bush, President George W. Bush, Governor
Jeb Bush and Marc at the annual RNC Bush Family Round Up,
Irving, Texas (2008), (Courtesy of Reflections Photography)

Tegra and Marc at the White House for Christmas with
Mrs. Laura and President George W. Bush (2008), (Courtesy
of the Office of President George W. Bush)

Tegra and Marc with President Bush at an RNC Regents event, Napa Valley, California (2008), (Courtesy of Reflections Photography)

Hon. Condoleezza Rice, Carly Fiorina, Marc Little, Bel Air, California (2010), (Courtesy of Nathanson's Photography)

Clarence Thomas, Associate Justice, United States
Supreme Court and Marc in chambers (2011)

Vice Presidential Candidate and Congressman Paul Ryan and Marc,
Los Angeles, California, (Courtesy of David Balfour Photography)

# Chapter 6:

## A Letter to the Family

*Take up your bed, and walk.*
*—Jesus the Christ, John 5:8*

I attended the inaugural production of August Wilson's *Two Trains Running* at the Ebony Repertory Theatre in Los Angeles under the direction of Wren Troy Brown. The play was brilliantly performed by actors Glynn Turman and Russell Hornsby, and I found its themes relevant to the challenges facing black America.

Turman's lead character, Memphis, is a restaurant owner who has lost a plot of land he'd purchased in the South before moving to Pittsburgh. When his restaurant is threatened by the city's powers of eminent domain, he fights for his rights and wins much more than the original $15,000 offered. Inspired by that victory at the end of the play, Memphis is determined to return to the South to win back his lost property there.

In a closing scene, his Aunt Esther asks him, "What's the sense of running into the end zone? You ain't got the ball." To finish well, you must go back to where you dropped the ball and pick it up. Only then can you win the game. At the play's climax, Memphis goes back to fight for his land.

Black Americans have collectively dropped the ball. That is not to say that there are not thousands of black men and women in higher education, young professionals, business owners and operators, and even the wealthiest among us today. Blacks are major contributors to the economic engine of this country and are among the brightest. Single black mothers are the heroines in the black community today. I salute them all, including my mother. However, the black community underachieves compared with other ethnic groups. For blacks to get in the game, we must go back and pick up the balls we dropped. We must reclaim our heritage. Church, education, responsible fatherhood, marriage, and support for one another are values we must once again embrace as a community. And we certainly must abandon our dependence on government handouts and return to being a community that controls its own destiny.

This also was the message of a concerned white Democrat back in 1965 on the eve of the War on Poverty. In March of that year, Assistant Secretary of Labor Daniel Patrick Moynihan, a future US senator, made the argument to President Lyndon B. Johnson in *The Negro Family: The Case for National Action*, commonly referred to as the Moynihan Report, when he said that "the heart of the deterioration of the fabric of Negro society is the deterioration of the Negro family. It is the fundamental source of the weakness of the Negro community at the present time."[1]

Moynihan understood that the black nuclear family could not survive being led by black women in a patriarchal society, and he called for a national response to the problem. He wrote,

What then is [the] problem? We feel the answer is clear enough. Three centuries of injustice have brought about deep-seated structural distortions in the life of the Negro American. At this point, the present tangle of pathology is capable of perpetuating itself without assistance from the white world. The cycle can be broken only if these distortions are set right.

In a word, a national effort towards the problems of Negro Americans must be directed towards the question of family structure. The object should be to strengthen the Negro family so as to enable it to raise and support its members as do other families. After that, how this group of Americans chooses to run its affairs, take advantage of its opportunities, or fail to do so, is none of the nation's business.[2]

It is as if the Moynihan Report were written today. Moynihan was excoriated for shedding light on the truth and was labeled a racist, but I believe he was a prophet. He warned against government subsidies and promoted addressing the underlying problems of the black family.

Moynihan argued that "without access to jobs and the means to contribute meaningful support to a family, black men would become systematically alienated from their roles as husbands and fathers. This would cause rates of divorce, abandonment, and out-of-wedlock births to skyrocket in the black community (a trend that had already begun by the mid-1960s)—leading to vast increases in the numbers of female-headed households and the high rates of poverty, low educational outcomes, and inflated rates of abuse that are associated with them. Moynihan made a compelling contemporary argument for the provision of jobs, job programs, vocational training, and educational programs for the black community."[3] Few listened, and we now are confronted with the consequences.

For many years, my father lived in a beautiful community in Santa Barbara, California. I visited him there often and enjoyed the coastal scene that always included flocks of seagulls, screeching and feeding along the shore. On one of my last trips there, I noticed that the seagulls were nowhere to be heard or seen.

"The seagulls had become dependent on the fishermen to feed them when they brought their catches in to the harbor," my father said. "When the fishing season ended and the fish migrated elsewhere, the seagulls died. They'd apparently forgotten how to fish on their own."

Blacks are suffering the same fate as Santa Barbara's seagulls. So many blacks have become dependent on government handouts that they have turned lethargic and have forgotten how to fend for themselves, just as Moynihan predicted.

Look around. In 2008, five million families occupied government-subsidized housing. Blacks make up 44 percent of the families in such housing. Blacks are 13.5 percent of the population but make up 67 percent of the 21.8 million children being raised by single mothers compared with 24 percent for whites.[4] We are the leaders in broken marriages. A disappointing 63.5 percent of blacks earned high school diplomas in the 2008-2009 Academic Year, compared with 82 percent of whites. Blacks are more than 40 percent of the prison population, and more than 70 percent of black inmates were raised by single mothers compared with 17 percent of white inmates. Finally, sixteen million black babies have been aborted since 1973 that we know of, and teen pregnancy is at an all-time high; little black girls are two times more likely to be pregnant than little white girls.[5]

All of these numbers point to one thing: blacks, as a community, have dropped the ball. We have little or no leadership in our homes, in our communities, or in the church house. No one is paying attention, and few are leading.

Black leaders and intellectuals have debated for nearly a hundred years whether black Americans should follow the teachings of Booker T. Washington or those of W.E.B. Du Bois. The more militant Du Bois advocated "persistent agitation, political action, and academic education" as the means for achieving full citizenship. A leader of the NAACP, Du Bois believed that the most educated blacks—the talented tenth—would lead the rest of the blacks in America through political action.

Washington, on the other hand, was seen as a compromiser who championed black self-determination through education, employment, and building personal wealth. Washington, a Republican, felt that once blacks established themselves as a force in the economy, they would earn respect from whites and win their civil rights.

The black community overwhelmingly followed the Du Bois model, and it landed us, in large part, where we are today. We are heavy in political action but light in economic success. Washington got it right. Self-reliance through education and employment leading to personal wealth is the cornerstone of a majority of the success stories in this nation. Not one community or individual has succeeded because the government wrote a welfare check. Perhaps people taking government money kept a roof over their heads, but just getting by is no substitute for economic freedom.

We have to make a choice as individuals to place value on important things like education, marriage, work ethic and economic independence. Only then can we succeed as a community. The examples of success are all around us—community by community, brown face by brown face, yellow face by yellow face, white face by white face, and black face by black face. But we have work to do. Uncle Sam doesn't have the plan to deliver blacks to the promised land. Destiny is what we make it; it is within the grasp of our own two hands and under the soles of our own two feet. But we must do the work just like the apostle Peter.

King Herod arrested and jailed Peter, intending to kill him. Herod had just killed James, the brother of John, by the sword. It did not look good for Peter, the giant upon whom Christ built His church. The Bible tells us that the night before Peter was to be brought to trial, the church was praying. On that night, Peter was sleeping between two soldiers. He was bound with two chains while sentries stood guard at the entrance of the jail. Acts 12:7–12 says,

Suddenly an angel of the Lord appeared and a light shone in the cell. He struck Peter on the side and woke him up. "Quick, get up!" he said, and the chains fell off Peter's wrists.

Then the angel said to him, "Put on your clothes and sandals." And Peter did so. "Wrap your cloak around you and follow me," the angel told him.

Peter followed him out of the prison, but he had no idea that what the angel was doing was really happening; he thought he was seeing a vision.

They passed the first and second guards and came to the iron gate leading to the city. It opened for them by itself, and they went through it. When they had walked the length of one street, suddenly the angel left him.

Then Peter came to himself and said, "Now I know without a doubt that the Lord sent his angel and rescued me from Herod's clutches and from everything the Jewish people were anticipating."

When this had dawned on him, he went to the house of Mary the mother of John, also called Mark, where many people had gathered and were praying.[6]

Even with the favor of God, our walk with Him is a partnership. We have our part to play. Here, Peter was miraculously delivered from jail and an imminent death, but even in the midst of his miracle, Peter had to put on his clothes and his sandals; he had to walk from his chains; he had to walk through the now-open jail bars, and then out into the street. God did not transport Peter to safety. Peter had to walk to his deliverance and he had to keep walking. He didn't look back.

Blacks must come to themselves, pursue opportunity along with everyone else, and not look back.

# Get on the Highway of Opportunity

Scores of minority groups—from the Jews to the Germans, the Italians, the Irish, the Asians, and even the Africans—have navigated the highway of opportunity called America and have achieved the American dream on their own.

The highway is long and wide. On the highway of opportunity, families cram into one car, twenty-deep, and travel together; they pile into one-bedroom apartments and sleep on the floor in order to realize the American dream. They have a plan as a family unit or community; they pool their earnings, they share their expenses, they help one another, and they all succeed together. It is an everyday occurrence in America—except in the black community.

Yes, blacks are on the highway of opportunity. However, they are not in the cars traveling the congested road; instead they are on the shoulder of the highway, many with their arms outstretched, palms up and heads down, waiting for Uncle Sam to take care of them. Many demand handouts, calling this "social justice." And indeed Uncle Sam responds. He brings the check but leaves blacks sitting right where he found them. Blacks did not listen to Gil Scott Heron. The train from Washington is a hundred years overdue. Wake up. It's not coming.

# What Does Social Justice Really Mean?

Far too many black men and women are still waiting on the curb for the "social justice" movement to rescue them when they should be dusting themselves off and making their own way. Social justice is the so-called offspring of the civil rights movement and Dr. Martin Luther King Jr. Who could ever oppose seeking social justice? But what does that term mean? It sounds good, doesn't it? Who would not be an advocate for social justice?

The desire for social justice is rooted in Judeo-Christian teachings and the tenets of other prominent and ancient religions. For example, Judaism teaches an obligation to perform charitable and philanthropic acts, while Catholic social teaching focuses on the sanctity of human life and the inherent dignity of every person.[6] These principles came to be called *social teachings*. The term *social justice* was first adopted in the early nineteenth century by the Catholic scholar and Jesuit Luigi Taparelli D'Azeglio. These religious philosophies all encourage care for the poor, among the most vulnerable of any society, in response to one's obedience to a moral code.

No one should disagree with the desire to help those among us who suffer in poverty. All of us have roles to play in attacking that problem; I believe there is even a limited role for government to play in the fight against poverty. Unfortunately, secular forces have hijacked the biblical principle of feeding and clothing the poor and have turned that philanthropic impulse into something else.

Social justice, a secular concept originating in the late twentieth century with philosopher John Rawls, now means creating a society based on human rights and equality rooted in economic egalitarianism. Economic egalitarianism is a state of economic affairs in which equality of outcome, as opposed to equality of opportunity, has been manufactured for all the participants of a society. It is a founding principle of various forms of socialism, communalism, and cooperative economic organization.[7]

Economic egalitarianism achieves equality of outcome through progressive taxation, income redistribution, and property redistribution, all of which are an assault on individual freedom.

"In fact, since the program of social justice inevitably involves claims for government provision of goods [like health care], paid for through the efforts of others, the term actually refers to an intention to use *force* to acquire one's desires. Not to *earn* desirable goods by rational thought and action, production and voluntary exchange, but to go in there and forcibly take goods from those who can supply them!"[9]

This is not about justice for the poor or the needy in our society. It's about social engineering. It is a move toward socialism.

A closer look reveals that "social justice" movement is just more of the same rhetoric that has done the black community no good. The term has been hijacked by the left. No longer a religious or secular philanthropic effort to do good, social justice teaches that "American society is an inherently 'oppressive' society that is 'systemically' 'racist', 'sexist,' and 'classist' and thus discriminates institutionally against women, nonwhites, working Americans, and the poor."[10]

"Social justice" preachers want us to concentrate on our nation's past mistakes rather than on its many remarkable accomplishments, such as electing the first black president; they emphasize problems and injustices rather than achievements.

"Social justice" does not mean *justice* as most Americans understand the term in a courtroom sense of the word. Those who use the term make clear that it means the United States is an unjust and oppressive society and that the solution is for community organizers to galvanize the poor and minorities to demonstrate and demand political power so they will be given government handouts.[11]

Yes, government handouts. Proponents of "social justice" want bigger government so that all citizens can be taken care of by government alone. It's not enough for the poor to be on the government dole—everyone else should be, too. Let's take from the rich and pass the money on to those who didn't earn it. Let's just quadruple society's problems by extending welfare to everyone. Huh? The flaw in the movement's logic is that eventually there will be no one left with enough wealth for the government to tax. Who will take care of the poor and vulnerable then?

This ideology is the new enemy of the black community. Yes, an enemy. This ideology turns the term *self-reliance* into a slur. Don't work for your own prosperity; let the government take care of you, because you have been oppressed. This is the antithesis of biblical principle. The Bible teaches, "If you don't work you don't eat … we command them to get to work immediately—no excuses, no arguments—and earn their keep … don't slack off in doing your duty."[12]

In other words, work is a divine requirement. It is not right to claim that someone else owes you an income that you did not earn. It's a lie. Don't believe it. The federal government owes us an equal opportunity to pursue freedom; it doesn't owe us equality of results. Income is not a right or an entitlement and is certainly not guaranteed. Wealth and prosperity come only through hard work.

# A Note to Fathers

Our society has fallen apart because men are not leading in their homes. Again, I dare not say that all black homes are in trouble; they are not, obviously. However, as in the story of the Pied Piper, the children of today have lost their way because daddy is not paying attention. In many cases, these children are dying.

Your daughter has been molested under your watch, and maybe even by you. Your daughter is looking for attention from other men, even strangers, because you're never home. Your daughter gravitates toward verbally and physically abusive relationships because you cussed at and beat her mother and taught her that it is all right to be abused. Now she accepts it as her own fate. She even confuses that example with love. Yes, she thinks being hit by her boyfriend or husband is what love looks like. That's what you taught her by your example.

Your daughter has multiple children though she is barely twenty years old because she tried to replace you with other men and had no sex education to prevent her pregnancies. She has to work to feed herself and her children now. But because you didn't teach her to value education, she's down at the local strip club dancing naked for dollars, or she is in a bar selling her body for fifty dollars. She doesn't believe she has any value because you taught her she was not worth your time; she has turned to other women for affection; she is now an alcoholic or crack head. Because she doesn't value herself, she could never value the lives of the multiple babies she has aborted. It's all because you were not there to love her. Now our community is dying because your daughter is dying.

Your son is ice cold. His eyes are empty and he cannot feel the pain anymore. He sees his mother with bruises on her face that you gave her. He was too young to protect her from you, so he feels worthless and impotent. He has no self-esteem; he believes he is a failure. Your son cannot get a job because he now has a record for doing petty crimes in the neighborhood with his friends, who kept him in trouble with the law. You weren't there to keep him at home at night. He aspires to be like the local kingpin on the corner who has all the money and the girls. That's all he can aspire to; without any education, it's the only model he has.

Your son sees women as sex objects. He is unable to communicate or connect with them in any real way. He's distant because he has never seen a healthy and loving male-female relationship. He hasn't learned how to respect a woman, but he loves his mother—the only woman he can relate to. Your son never sees the children he fathered because he doesn't know how to be a father. He's scared to try. He doesn't want to fail at anything else. Why try? You never showed him how to be daddy; you were never there. Now our community is dying because your son is dying.

Fathers, there are three principles to saving your family. If you begin today, there is still hope.

# Pay Attention

Fathers, all your daughter really needs is for you to be present. Show up. Tell her how special she is, how smart she is, how talented she is. Women and girls blossom with very simple gestures. Hold your daughter's hand; smile at her; sit her on your lap, no matter how old she is, and tell her you love her. Do it often. That will change her life. Show her how she should be treated by treating her mother well, with respect. All of your daughter's relationships with men will be based on how you interact with her mother and on whether she has a healthy, loving father-daughter relationship. If you don't have a healthy and loving relationship with your daughter, she will be on the stripper pole soon enough. It's your choice. That's right—*your* choice.

Your son needs to see you lead. He needs to see a model of male leadership. If you don't provide a model, someone else will. The streets are right outside, willing to be his dad. Your model must include discipline. Boys need structure; if boys don't have structure, they will never understand boundaries. A boy who doesn't understand boundaries will rape and kill. Discipline and structure are critical.

Your model must include a work ethic. Boys need to value hard work. If you don't work, you don't eat, the Bible says. Your model must include spending time with him. Boys also need to value recreation. Life is not all work and no play. Recreation instills balance and socialization.

Your model also must include how to be responsible. A boy needs to value being responsible for something or someone other than himself. Although his nature is to provide, he must understand how to go about it. Your son, father, is the key to the future of your family. If you don't raise him right, the future is dead. Your model must include financial literacy. Teach the basics like: don't worship money, don't spend more than you make, and save for a rainy day. Then add the simple things. Always look the person you're talking to in the eye; that means you can be trusted. Always give a firm handshake; that is a sign of strong character. Keep your word. If you say it, then mean it. Fathers, *pay attention*.

Paying attention means being generous with your time. Organize yourself around the emotional, physical, and psychological needs of your family. Your time is like the blood coursing through the veins of your family. If you give it, your family will live.

My father has always been one to give of his time. He taught by example the value of sharing yourself with others.

Recently, as a Hall of Famer, he was a guest at the Daniel Gram Foundation in Denver where he spoke to several classes of high school students. Students from the Lookout Mountain School for Boys in Denver were among those invited. One seventeen-year-old boy, Mike, asked if he could meet with my father on Friday night, time permitting. Of course, my Dad said yes.

Unfortunately, time ran short that day, so Mike didn't get the chance to speak with his hero. Mike returned to school that night unsatisfied.

He persisted. He asked for permission to return to the nearby high school football field where he met Mr. Little so he could have that conversation he longed for. Luckily, the headmaster allowed him to return.

Mike raced back early the next day to find Floyd Little. "Mr. Little, Mr. Little," he said as he spotted him in the auditorium, ending a conversation. "You promised yesterday we could speak. Do you have time?" Mike asked.

Of course, my father was more than willing to spend time with the black teenager who hungered for a few moments with him.

Mike told my father his dream of being a running back himself one day. He had gotten into some trouble by robbing a local pharmacy. His foray into a life of crime landed him at the boys school, and he needed some advice. "How can I turn my life around, Mr. Little?" he asked. "I just need direction."

He was longing for a word from a man he didn't even know but respected.

My Dad responded as he always does. He welled up with emotion and poured out encouragement. My father always taught me to dream big. "Have big dreams," he'd always say. "Shoot for the moon. Even if you miss, you'll land among the stars. Have big dreams."

His chat with Mike was no different. "Mike," he said, "ninety percent of the running backs in the NFL are under six feet tall and under two hundred pounds." Mike, five feet nine and 180 pounds, didn't think he was big enough to be a running back. Little did he know that he was talking to a guy whose coaches and teammates always said he was not big enough to play. "You can do it, Mike. You can do it," my dad said.

By the time Mike's conversation with my dad was over, he had a new friend and a commitment from my father not only to keep up with him, but also to provide one of Denver's finest law firms to attend his court hearing.

I suspect the seed of time my dad sowed into Mike's life that day will grow into a gigantic tree. I suspect Mike will never be the same, and neither will the community he joins.

Imagine if Mike had a father who was present in his life and spent quality time with him. How his life could be changed daily!

# Be Caring

The claim that men are not emotional is a lie. We are emotional, but we refuse to share that side of ourselves. Scared that we may be perceived as weak, we mask our feelings. Masking your feelings confuses your daughter because she is unsure of how daddy really feels; masking your feelings around your daughter provides a false model in her dealings with other men. Masking your feelings with your son teaches him to keep his feelings to himself just like you do.

My father and I have a very open and emotional relationship. We understand that tomorrow is not promised, so we live each day as if it could be our last. We value our time together, and we say how we feel because we may never get the chance again. When you understand the gift of life and the gift of true friendship, you cannot take it for granted. When we share, very often we cry. Life is too precious not to share your emotions, how you feel, with the people you love.

My father and I set a new paradigm on August 5, 2010, the day Dad was enshrined in the Pro Football Hall of Fame. The ceremony was viewed by millions of people around the world. Dad gave me the honor to speak for our entire family and present him for induction. Dad had been waiting thirty-five years for this moment; it was preceded by a great deal of pain and disappointment that the Hall of Fame voters had overlooked him. And now, here we were standing on the stage for the Pro Football Hall of Fame enshrinement. Here is what I said:

> Floyd Little can often be heard saying, "I do not choose to be a common man. It is my right to be uncommon—if I can." That's my dad—an uncommon man.
>
> My name is Marc Little, and I have the honor of speaking on behalf of my sisters, Christy and Kyra, and our entire family.
>
> Today is an extraordinary day for us, but we know that Floyd Little enters the Pro Football Hall of Fame riding on the coattails of uncommon giants.
>
> He rode on the coattails of a mother who raised him and five siblings in the city of New Haven, Connecticut; she supported Dad's athletic prowess as a way to make it out of New Haven. I believe Gramma Little is looking down from heaven and is proud today.
>
> He rode on the coattails of a colleague, Ernie Davis, who recruited him to Syracuse University where they both became the standard-bearers for the number forty-four along with the inimitable Jim Brown.
>
> And finally, Dad rode on the coattails of a dear friend, Val Pinchbeck, whose mission was to see him inducted into the Hall but who had a heart attack and passed away while crossing a street in New York. Val, I dare say, would be filled with joy today.
>
> I honor these uncommon giants.

They all saw something special in Floyd Little, but as a student he was told he was not smart enough; as an athlete he was told he was not tall enough or big enough to make a difference; but Floyd Little had a calling to greatness, a divine call that predestined this very moment to shine the light today as evidence that in spite of the limitations others place on us, we can do all things through Christ, who strengthens us.

He ran around those teachers who said he would never make it, and he emerged a giant. Dad has been known to be a leader ever since. When he arrived in Denver as a rookie, he was made captain. The team, destined to leave the city, remained because of Floyd Little. They called him "The Franchise" because of it. His leadership impacted our family as well. My sisters and I are all college graduates today. That's success; that's Dad's legacy.

But year after year, a nomination to the Hall of Fame eluded my dad.

Then one day in August 2008, Joe Biden appeared in IN-VESCO Field for the Democratic National Convention before eighty-four thousand attendees and thirty-eight million television viewers and said, "Denver is Floyd Little's town; I thought I would be standing here with my old friend, Floyd Little."

I called Dad and said, "God just reached out of eternity and into the present and spoke to you through Joe Biden and said, 'Floyd, I hear your prayers and I see you.'" I believed with all my heart that my father's prayers to be recognized among the best to ever play the game would soon be answered. And indeed they were.

Yes, Dad, God does see you and He loves you. Your hard work, your blood, sweat, and tears as a player and even as a father were not in vain. Congratulations. You are the wind beneath our wings.

Now, ladies and gentlemen, please join me in presenting to the Pro Football Hall of Fame, a giant of humanity, an uncommon man, my hero, my best friend, my dad, Floyd Little.

After I gave the presentation speech, Dad and I unveiled his bust, which will be forever displayed in Canton, Ohio. After we pulled the veil off of the bust, we hugged and as usual, we pecked (kissed) each other right on the mouth! Michael Irving, the commentator for ESPN and Hall of Famer himself, remarked on air, "The next time my son does something I approve of, I'm going to kiss him right in the mouth, too!" Irving's reaction to our show of affection was shared by many. Seeing a father and son openly share their love for one another was a new model, one that our communities can benefit from.

Floyd and Marc at the Pro Football Hall of Fame jacket
ceremony, Canton, Ohio (2010), (Courtesy of Daryn Hollis)

Floyd and Marc at the Pro Football Hall of Fame bust unveiling
ceremony, Canton, Ohio (2010), (Courtesy of Daryn Hollis)

Floyd and Marc, Pro Football Hall of Fame Museum,
Canton, Ohio (2010), (Courtesy of Daryn Hollis)

Fan appreciation

# Set a Godly Standard

Demonstrate God's model for love in your home. God says that you are the priest in your home. Love your wife as Christ loves the church. Leading means you set the standard, you go first, you show the way. You are supposed to lead in love, lead in making decisions, lead in providing for your family, lead in securing your home and family, lead in making preparations, and lead in prayer. Lead in all things. When a man leads in the right way, a godly woman is happy to support him. A man who leads has a family following him.

Leadership, for a man, is akin to shining like the sun. When the sun shines, the flowers bloom. As the flowers bloom, the sun shines.

One gives back to the other in a continuous exchange. That's God's model of leadership in your home, and, men, it begins with you.

The Bible says, "Train a child in the way he should go and when he is older he will not depart from it."[13] In an unspiritual context, this passage means garbage in, garbage out. You get out what you put in.

You cannot expect to open a money market bank account, make no deposit, and then earn and withdraw interest. No. You can earn interest only on what you've deposited.

So, men, if you don't provide leadership in your home, you cannot expect to receive an inheritance or legacy from your seed. You must make the investment.

# A Note to Sons and Daughters

Many of you have traveled very difficult roads and lived very difficult lives in terms of your relationships with your mothers and fathers. You may be well educated and successful; you may be happily married with a beautiful family. But you may still be wounded by a mother, father, or family member.

Many daughters, as they grow older, have love-hate relationships with their mothers. Envy and strife plague many mother-daughter relationships.

Many sons and daughters have grown up without a father in the home. Many have been sexually molested and otherwise physically or verbally abused over the years. Others have simply been neglected. You may feel a major void in your heart, and it hurts because your father never seemed to care for you or about you.

The decisions you've made in your life to this point have been made out of the loneliness and pain from your relationship with your mother or father. You are so comfortable with living in a dysfunctional relationship that you don't even dwell on it anymore. It's the thorn in your side that no longer seems to bother you. You've developed a callous over your heart to avoid the pain.

You have to deal with that relationship. The pain of that relationship will cripple you and affect every relationship you have, including with your own children. Here are some things to consider in resolving some of your relationship challenges with your parents or other members of your family.

# Forgiveness

Parents are struggling or dealing with their own pasts, their own decisions, and their own fears. Not everything that your mother and father did as your parents was directed at you. Rather, it was a response to their own lack of education and understanding or their own circumstance.

If you can begin to understand that even your own parents are flawed and not the perfect people you hoped them to be, you can begin to put yourself in their shoes and forgive them. The decisions they made that hurt you were not necessarily about you. Try understanding and forgiveness.

My mother gave me the surname of the very caring man who decided to marry her when I was born. He was not my father. My mother, out of respect for him, I guess, gave me his last name, Thomas. I carried that name all the way until middle school when I realized that I wanted to bear my biological father's name, Little.

Later in life, I wanted to alter my birth certificate to reflect the correct information and the prospect of the process was unnerving. But with some thought, I quickly appreciated what my mother must have been going through facing single parenthood. She did what she believed was right at the time. Most of all, she kept me. With careful thought and appreciation, how could I not understand her decision? How could I spend any time pondering the grief it was causing me to make the necessary changes to my name? It wasn't just about me and wasn't all that important at the end of the day. Her circumstances dictated her choices, and she did a great job.

Practice understanding and get forgiveness.

# Be Big About It

Parents don't always behave like mature adults. As a son or daughter, you may very well be more emotionally equipped than your mother, father, or other family member to deal with the hurtful things of the past. You may be better equipped to mediate issues as well.

You may have to be the one to go to your relative and start the conversation. Put your cards on the table, and tell your mother or father how you feel. Explain your hurt in a loving, non-argumentative, and mature voice. (Repeat: non-argumentative.) Get it all out. Stop being the child and be an adult about it.

# Acceptance

Not every problem has a solution, and not every person can listen to reason and make the appropriate adjustments in relationships.

As a son or daughter, you may simply have to accept your relatives for who and what they are. With understanding, you may have to accept those things about them or about the past that you cannot change.

It sounds easy, but it isn't. However, by acknowledging the issue, by voicing your awareness of it, you can then move on in clarity and understanding.

You will find peace.

# Unconditional love

Love your relative with the heart of Christ. In Corinthians, the apostle Paul teaches us what unconditional love looks like:

> Love is patient, love is kind. It does not envy, it does not boast, it is not proud. It is not rude, it is not self-seeking, it is not easily angered, it keeps no record of wrongs. Love does not delight in evil but rejoices with the truth. It always protects, always trusts, always hopes, always perseveres. Love never fails.[14]

We constantly say we love each other. In fact, the use of the words *I love you* is almost as common as *hi* and *good-bye*. Do we really understand what love looks like?

If you love your mother and father with the unconditional love of Christ, you will hold no record of wrongs against them. You will see them as Christ sees them: as sinners, flawed, and in need of His love and salvation. Try to see your broken and flawed mother and father as Christ sees them.

Let your healing begin!

# Chapter 7:

## A Challenge to the Republican Party

*Continuous effort—not strength or intelligence—*
*is the key to unlocking our potential.*
*—Winston Churchill*

In the story of the Pied Piper, the rat catcher leads the children, the future of the village, to their deaths.

Our elected officials are modern-day Pied Pipers with the power to save or destroy the future of our great nation. They persuasively play their fifes and entice our communities to blindly follow them. We rarely, if ever, ask them tough questions unless they're Republicans; we never challenge their leadership even though they have the power to make policy that changes lives forever.

It is no secret that the Republican Party lost the votes of blacks long ago. I chronicle the loss of that vote in chapter 3. Blacks started deserting the party with the Great Compromise of 1877 and just about completely left with the civil rights legislation of 1964 and 1965. It is high time the GOP shared the blame for the black community's decline for failing to fight the damaging policies of the past.

Notwithstanding Republicans' push to bring about welfare reform under the Clinton administration and No Child Left Behind under George W. Bush, they have simply not done enough. It's not enough to decry the failed policies of the Democratic Party and the deleterious impact they've had on the black community. It's time the GOP made the black community a priority. It's time to challenge our conservative and Republican leaders and demand that the Party of Lincoln return to its roots, as liberal as they may have been, and steer blacks away from crippling entitlement programs and failed leadership to responsible leadership and a pathway to economic freedom. Here are a few thoughts on how to do that.

# Fiscal Responsibility

Our country, and therefore the world, is on the brink of financial disaster. With the spending of the Obama administration, we've amassed $16 trillion of debt to pass on to our grandchildren. Republicans must fight to stem the tide of increased federal government spending and get our financial house in order. With the pending collapse of the European Union, assuming Germany cannot save it, the world is circling the drain. We are the only hope.

A few thoughts for the GOP to focus on: get rid of the Department of Education and return education to the states; reduce the size of the civilian federal work force by a large percentage; repeal or defund ObamaCare but make health insurance more affordable across the country by making health insurance portable across state lines and allow insurance plans to compete across state lines; minimize the need for doctors to practice defensive medicine by implementing meaningful tort reform; return the $719 billion to Medicare raided by the Obama administration to help pay for ObamaCare; reduce the individual, corporate and capital gains tax brackets to generate income like Reagan did in the 80's; repeal the death tax so that our hard work is not taxed twice; and finally overhaul Medicare, Medicaid, and Social Security. They are all bankrupt. What are we waiting for?

The road toward fiscal responsibility is a long one; unfortunately, conservatives (Republican and/or Democrat) are the only ones who understand that America cannot spend its way out of this recession. The spending of the past four years alone under the Obama administration has put the nation in harm's way. It's time to reverse course.

# Jobs

In their pursuit of employment, blacks and Latinos in California are disproportionately burdened by nonviolent-felony records. As with bankruptcy or other negative credit reporting, the state legislatures should sunset (expunge) any nonviolent-felony record three years after the date of conviction and after restitution has been made. This would empower those who have learned from their mistakes, reduce recidivism, and allow these men and women employment opportunities unaffected by the stigma of a felonious past.[1]

Nearly two-thirds of the people released from prison served time for nonviolent offenses including drug (37 percent) and property (25 percent) offenses. Two out of three of those released are people of color: 48 percent African American and 25 percent Latino.

Sun setting these records would signal real change for the black community—change to believe in!

# Illegal Immigration

Because of the open border and sanctuary city policies of the US and certain large cities, illegal immigration is disproportionately impacting the black labor force. We must secure our borders and implement a guest worker program that helps control the flow of immigration and impose large fines to employers who hire illegal workers. Illegal immigration must be abated. Enforce the federal laws so that states won't have to do the federal government's job.

# School Choice

The GOP must continue to promote school choice programs for kindergarten through twelfth grade to allow students to transfer out of poor-performing public schools and into private schools through vouchers and tax credits at the state level. Research demonstrates that this not only increases the graduation rate for students but increases competition among public schools. The Pell Grants for Kids Program proposed by George W. Bush is a good idea that will help students in every state.

# Public School Reform

The GOP can be instrumental in ensuring that teachers are evaluated and retain employment based on their ability to get results in the classroom, and not just because they have tenure or union protection. Do away with tenure where possible so that merit is the only factor for teachers remaining employed.

Reform urban teacher preparation programs to find and equip teachers in a practical, hands-on environment for the tough urban experiences they will face, with the ultimate goal of academic achievement that prepares students to compete in a global society.

Create a competitive atmosphere in the founding spirit of charter schools. Schools that don't cut it are given a short time to improve, and if they don't, are closed. Schools that do well can share best practices with average and below-average schools to assist them in their improvement.

# Oppose Punishing the Preaching of the Gospel

Preemptively oppose the likes of H.R. 1592 (passed in the House in May 2007) and S. 1105 (failed in the Senate in September 2007), which would have made it a hate crime for pastors to preach that the practice of homosexuality is a sin. Standing up to such legislation would open doors to conservative black pastors and others as opposed to recent efforts by Senator Chuck Grassley to investigate the finances of certain televangelists because of the appearance of prosperity. This is not the right course.

# Get Back to Family Values: The Social Issues

Presidential campaigns now abandon the call to family values. Judeo-Christian values are under assault all across the nation, but no Politician makes this a national issue. The social conservative voice is dying in this country, and no political party or church is speaking up to prevent this from happening. It was only by happenstance that conversations about contraception and the intersection of government and faith took place during the 2012 Republican presidential primary campaign and presidential contender Rick Santorum the only flag waver. Otherwise, no one seems to believe a godly standard is important anymore. The Republican Party has lost its core. While it is important that the GOP expand to attract more diverse support, Judeo-Christian values must be restored as the party's foundation. Let's put godliness on the political agenda again.

The GOP can promote traditional family values in the following ways: 1) Value marriage. It is proven that two-parent households are more successful than single-parent households. Traditional marriage can be supported, as it is, with tax incentives, and by continuing to stand for traditional marriage between one man and one woman. 2) Value education. As stated above, promote school voucher programs, charter schools and teachers union reform. Education has lost its place as the core and foundation of success in America. It must be restored as the single most important thing for families to achieve. 3) Value the sanctity of human life. Federal tax dollars must not be used to fund the murder of the unborn (e.g. defund Planned Parenthood) and *Roe v. Wade* should be overturned. 16 million black babies alone have been aborted since 1973. This is genocide and no one is noticing. Extreme measures should be taken to save the lives of the unborn. 4) Value religious freedom. Don't let a minority agenda force a false argument that conservatives have waged a war against women by denying them access to birth control as they have done in the 2012 presidential election. Birth control is readily available for cheap across this country nor should my tax dollars be used to subsidize birth control. What we must not allow is the coercion of our religious institutions to pay for contraception under their health insurance plans in violation of their religious beliefs. Enough is enough. The real war against women is waged by the media who promote television shows, ads, movies, and videos exploiting the sexuality of our young women and sending the message that being slutty and promiscuous is somehow a a good thing. The war against women is most tangible in the Middle East and Africa where women are still second class citizens in many of those societies. Let's put the spot light on women who are truly under attack 5) Keep the faith. Fight the LGBT agenda bent on changing the curricula in our schools to teach awareness of homosexuality; fight the removal of prayer from the public square and refuse to deny our faith when called upon; promote the election of fellow believers to elected office; and remember that "faith provides the moral order that ties one generation to the next, and without which the civil society cannot survive."[2]

## Ask for Everyone's Vote

Pastors take a strange pride in announcing that Republicans do not come to their churches to ask for the black vote. By default, blacks no longer have to think about whom to vote for. It seems there is only one option—the Democrat. I believe that Republican leaders still regard minorities as strangers. Their lack of comfort with nonwhite voters perpetuates the myth.

White business leaders and the Republican Party continue to treat black America as if it were an alien nation. The GOP has a good product; it simply needs to package it, market it to everyone, and sell it!

I've tried to bridge that divide. I was a major donor to Senator John McCain and I've spoken with him. As the chief operating officer of a large arena in Inglewood, California at that time, I offered the the building to him for a rally. I also made him aware that the building is owned by a black church with a congregation of nearly thirteen thousand.

I thought the response would be swift. A call never came.

Since the Democratic convention of 1948 when some of the racist southern Democrats left the party to protest President Truman's civil rights agenda, joining the Republican Party, the GOP has been seen as racist by many blacks. Republicans have done little to reverse those feelings.

# Republicans Must Tell The Story

Sometimes you cannot just lead by example. You must also explain that your philosophies and values are beneficial for everyone. Self-determination is a conservative value that should have a strong appeal in a resurgent black America.

# GOP: Put Your Money Where Your Mouth Is

It does no good to say you want diversity while failing to provide financial support for black Republican candidates commensurate with nonblack candidates. The Bible says if you want to know where a man's heart is, find his treasure. The GOP can attract blacks and other minority voters if its heart is sincere. Support should be provided not only to candidates but to the African American Republican Leadership Council, Black America's Political Action Committee, the Center for New Black Leadership, the Harlem Republican Club, the Pinchback Society, and Project 21. These are just a handful of black organizations that if supported could promote and expand the agenda of the Republican National Committee and attract more black voters to the party. The GOP has to put its money and time into giving these organizations the strength needed to reverse the trend.

# The United States Supreme Court

One of my most recent highlights was visiting Associate Justice Clarence Thomas in his chambers. I wrote him a letter expressing my desire to meet and I quickly devoured his memoir, *My Grandfather's Son*. He quickly responded with an invitation. Not only did we meet, but we shared stories and camaraderie for more than two hours. He was amazingly affable and felt like the uncle I never had. Other than having a face-to-face with President George W. Bush, I cannot recall a more memorable encounter. Justice Thomas is a true conservative and an American hero.

After racing from his chambers with great delight, I couldn't wait to take notes of what we discussed so I would always remember. I recorded over 24 different topics of discussion from childhood experiences to sports. It turns out Justice Thomas is a fan of Floyd Little. Who knew.

In any event, Justice Thomas sits on the highest court in the land. The United States Supreme Court. And aside from the stories I can now share with my children and grandchildren, God willing, of our time together, he has played and will continue to play a part in shaping the American society and jurisprudence for generations to come.

Because each justice is appointed to a life term, it is critical that when Republicans occupy the Oval Office we nominate and confirm federal and Supreme Court justices who will strictly uphold and interpret the Constitution.

We have fallen into a season where the courts have become more activist-like and persuaded by public opinion. It is currently divided 5-4 typically and the scales can be tipped in either direction at any given time. We must avoid a court populated with politicians at all costs.

# Chapter 8:

## Are You a Democrat or a Republican? Take the Test

**B**eyond Red vs. Blue,[1] a political typology published on May 4, 2011, by the Pew Research Center, provides an update on trends among the voters who make up the political parties. It provides a wealth of research and a resource for those interested in the ideologies associated with the left and the right. It is included below.

Our great nation is not monolithic. We don't all think alike, but we are affected by our environment, our experiences, our friends and neighbors, and our common interests. We all have differing backgrounds that lead us to think and vote certain ways. Some of us are regular churchgoers, others are not. We live in very different areas of the country. Some of us are business owners, while others are blue-collar workers or other employees. All of these factors influence how we vote. The Pew Research Center does a great job of defining these political groups. With which political group do you most closely align? Read the descriptions below and then take the test by following the link at the end of this chapter.

# Staunch Conservatives

9% OF ADULT POPULATION /11% OF REGISTERED VOTERS

| ■ Democrat | ■ Indep-lean Dem | ■ Indep-no lean | ■ Indep-lean Rep | ■ Republican |
|---|---|---|---|---|

| 16 | 84 |
|---|---|

**Basic Description:** This extremely partisan Republican group is strongly conservative on economic and social policy and favors an assertive foreign policy. They are highly engaged in politics, most (72%) agree with the Tea Party, 54% regularly watch Fox News, and nearly half (47%) believe that President Obama was born outside the US.

**Defining values:** Extremely critical of the federal government and supportive of sharply limited government. Pro-business and strongly opposed to environmental regulation. Believe that military strength is the best way to ensure peace. Highly religious; most say homosexuality should be discouraged by society.

| KEY BELIEFS | General Public | Staunch Conservatives |
|---|---|---|
| | % | % |
| Government is almost always wasteful and inefficient | 55 | 90 |
| The best way to ensure peace is through military strength | 31 | 76 |
| Most corporations make a fair and reasonable profit | 39 | 78 |
| Stricter environmental laws and regulations cost too many jobs and hurt the economy | 39 | 92 |
| The government today can't afford to do much more to help the needy | 51 | 87 |
| New health care law will have a mostly bad effect on U.S. health care | 27 | 80 |
| Religion is a very important part of my life | 71 | 90 |
| The U.S. stands above all other countries in the world | 38 | 67 |
| The growing number of newcomers from other countries threatens traditional American customs and values | 39 | 68 |

PEW RESEARCH CENTER 2011 Political Typology.

**Who they are:** More than nine in ten (92%) non-Hispanic white and 56% male. The oldest of the groups (61% ages 50 and older). Married

(79%), Protestant (72%, including 43% white evangelical), and financially comfortable (70% say paying the bills is not a problem).

**Lifestyle notes:** Many are gun owners (57%) and regular churchgoers (57% attend weekly or more often), and fully 81% are homeowners. More watch Glenn Beck (23%) and listen to Rush Limbaugh (21%) than any other group.

# Main Street Republicans

11% OF ADULT POPULATION /14% OF REGISTERED VOTERS

**Basic Description:** Concentrated in the South and Midwest. Main Street Republicans differ from Staunch Conservatives in the degree of their conservatism and in their skepticism about business. They are socially and fiscally conservative but supportive of government efforts to protect the environment.

**Defining values:** Highly critical of government. Very religious and strongly committed to traditional social values. Generally negative about immigrants and mostly opposed to social welfare programs. But much less enamored of business than Staunch Conservatives and less supportive of an assertive foreign policy.

| KEY BELIEFS | General Public | Main Street Republicans |
|---|---|---|
| | % | % |
| Government is almost always wasteful and inefficient | 55 | 72 |
| The government today can't afford to do much more to help the needy | 51 | 75 |
| Most corporations make a fair and reasonable profit | 39 | 34 |
| Stricter environmental laws and regulations cost too many jobs and hurt the economy | 39 | 22 |
| Homosexuality should be discouraged by society | 33 | 60 |
| Religion is a very important part of my life | 71 | 91 |
| The growing number of newcomers from other countries threatens traditional American customs and values | 39 | 56 |
| The best way to ensure peace is through military strength | 31 | 39 |

PEW RESEARCH CENTER 2011 Political Typology.

**Who they are:** Predominantly non-Hispanic white (88%), with two-thirds living in the South (40%) or Midwest (27%). A majority are Protestant (65%, including 38% white evangelical). A large majority (69%) are generally satisfied financially.

**Lifestyle notes:** Most (84%) are homeowners. About half are gun owners (51%) and regular churchgoers (53% attend weekly or more often). Nearly a quarter (24%) follow NASCAR racing. About half (51%) watch network evening news.

# Libertarians

9% OF ADULT POPULATION /10% OF REGISTERED VOTERS

| ■ Democrat | ▨ Indep-lean Dem | ▨ Indep-no lean | ▨ Indep-lean Rep | ■ Republican |
|---|---|---|---|---|
| 5 | 6 | 12 | 49 | 28 |

**Basic Description:** This Republican-oriented, predominantly male group mostly conforms to the classic profile of the libertarian in its combination of strong economic conservatism and relatively liberal views on social issues. Much less religious than other GOP-oriented groups, Libertarians are relatively comfortable financially—nearly half (46%) say they are professional or business class, among the highest of the typology groups.

**Defining values:** Highly critical of government. Disapprove of social welfare programs. Pro-business and strongly opposed to regulation. Accepting of homosexuality. Moderate views about immigrants compared with other Republican-oriented groups.

| KEY BELIEFS | General Public | Libertarians |
|---|---|---|
| | % | % |
| Government is almost always wasteful and inefficient | 55 | 82 |
| The government today can't afford to do much more to help the needy | 51 | 85 |
| Most corporations make a fair and reasonable profit | 39 | 83 |
| Stricter environmental laws and regulations cost too many jobs and hurt the economy | 39 | 79 |
| Homosexuality should be discouraged by society | 33 | 19 |
| Religion is a very important part of my life | 71 | 53 |
| The growing number of newcomers from other countries threatens traditional American customs and values | 39 | 37 |
| Most people who want to get ahead can make it if they're willing to work hard | 62 | 80 |

PEW RESEARCH CENTER 2011 Political Typology.

**Who they are:** Most (85%) are non-Hispanic white and two-thirds (67%) are male. Well educated (71% have attended college) and affluent (39% have incomes of $75,000 or more).

**Lifestyle notes:** Less likely than other GOP groups to attend church weekly (26%). More than half (56%) use social networking sites, and 46% have a gun in the household; 54% currently have a US passport, 36% trade stocks, 38% regularly watch Fox News, and 17% regularly listen to NPR.

# Disaffecteds

11% OF ADULT POPULATION /11% OF REGISTERED VOTERS

| ■Democrat | ▩Indep-lean Dem | ▩Indep-no lean | ▩Indep-lean Rep | ■Republican |
|---|---|---|---|---|
| 9 | 31 | 35 | | 25 |

**Basic Description:** The most financially stressed of the eight typology groups, Disaffecteds are very critical of both business and government. They are sympathetic to the poor and supportive of social welfare programs. Most are skeptical about immigrants and doubtful that the US can solve its problems. They are pessimistic about their own financial future.

**Defining values:** A majority believe that the government is wasteful and inefficient and that regulation does more harm than good. But nearly all say too much power is concentrated in a few companies. Religious and socially conservative.

| KEY BELIEFS | General Public | Disaffecteds |
|---|---|---|
| | % | % |
| Government is almost always wasteful and inefficient | 55 | 73 |
| Most corporations make a fair and reasonable profit | 39 | 21 |
| I often don't have enough money to make ends meet | 43 | 83 |
| Religion is a very important part of my life | 71 | 84 |
| The government should do more to help needy Americans, even if it means going deeper into debt | 41 | 61 |
| Immigrants today are a burden on our country because they take our jobs, housing and health care | 44 | 64 |
| This country can't solve many of its important problems | 37 | 56 |
| We should pay less attention to problems overseas and concentrate on problems here at home | 58 | 73 |

PEW RESEARCH CENTER 2011 Political Typology.

**Who they are:** About three-quarters (77%) are non-Hispanic white and two-thirds (66%) have only a high school education or less. Compared with the national average, more are parents (44%). Fully 71% have experienced unemployment in their household in the past 12 months. About half (48%) describe their household as "struggling."

**Lifestyle notes:** Only 26% have a US passport, 23% follow NASCAR, and 41% did not vote in 2010.

# Post-Moderns

13% OF ADULT POPULATION /14% OF REGISTERED VOTERS

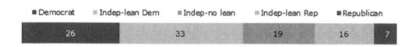

**Basic Description:** Well-educated and financially comfortable. Post-Moderns are supportive of many aspects of government though they take conservative positions on questions about racial policy and the social safety net. Very liberal on social issues. Post-Moderns were strong supporters of Barack Obama in 2008, but turned out at far lower rates in 2010.

**Defining values:** Strongly supportive of regulation and environmental protection. Favor the use of diplomacy rather than military force to ensure peace. Generally positive about immigrants and their contributions to society.

| KEY BELIEFS | General Public | Post-Moderns |
|---|---|---|
| | % | % |
| This country should do whatever it takes to protect the environment | 71 | 91 |
| The government should do more to help needy Americans, even if it means going deeper into debt | 41 | 27 |
| Our country needs to continue making changes to give blacks equal rights with whites | 45 | 25 |
| Religion is a very important part of my life | 71 | 42 |
| Homosexuality should be accepted by society | 58 | 91 |
| Wall Street helps the American economy more than it hurts | 38 | 56 |
| Good diplomacy is the best way to ensure peace | 58 | 76 |
| The growing number of newcomers from other countries strengthens American society | 52 | 71 |

PEW RESEARCH CENTER 2011 Political Typology.

**Who they are:** The youngest of the typology groups (32% under age 30); a majority are non-Hispanic white (70%) and have at least some college experience (71%). Nearly a third (31%) are unaffiliated with any religious tradition. Half live in either the Northeast (25%) or the West (25%). A majority (58%) lives in the suburbs.

**Lifestyle notes:** 63% use social networking. One in five (20%) regularly listen to NPR, 14% regularly watch *The Daily Show*, 10% read *The New York Times,* 31% trade stocks, and 53% have a passport.

# New Coalition Democrats

10% OF ADULT POPULATION /9% OF REGISTERED VOTERS

| ■ Democrat | Indep-lean Dem | Indep-no lean | Indep-lean Rep | ■Republican |
|---|---|---|---|---|
| 56 | | 25 | 14 | 3 2 |

**Basic Description:** This majority-minority group is highly religious and financially stressed. They are generally upbeat about both the country's ability to solve problems and an individual's ability to get ahead through hard work.

**Defining values:** Generally supportive of government, but divided over expanding the social safety net. Reflecting their own diverse makeup, they are pro-immigrant. Socially conservative, about as many say homosexuality should be discouraged as say it should be accepted.

| KEY BELIEFS | General Public | New Coalition Democrats |
|---|---|---|
| | % | % |
| Government regulation of business is necessary to protect the public interest | 47 | 77 |
| Would rather have a bigger government providing more services | 42 | 65 |
| The growing number of newcomers from other countries strengthens American society | 52 | 78 |
| Our country needs to continue making changes to give blacks equal rights with whites | 45 | 69 |
| Good diplomacy is the best way to ensure peace | 58 | 74 |
| Most corporations make a fair and reasonable profit | 39 | 53 |
| Homosexuality should be discouraged by society | 33 | 47 |
| Religion is a very important part of my life | 71 | 92 |

PEW RESEARCH CENTER 2011 Political Typology.

**Who they are:** Nearly equal proportions white (34%), black (30%), and Latino (26%); about three in ten (29%) are first- or second-generation

Americans; 55% have only a high school education or less. Nearly a quarter (23%) are not registered to vote.

**Lifestyle notes:** Half (50%) are regular volunteers for charity or nonprofit groups. More than a quarter (27%) are looking for work or would prefer a full-time job to the part-time job they hold. Only 34% read a daily newspaper. 25% regularly listen to NPR. 34% buy organic foods.

# Hard-Pressed Democrats

13% OF ADULT POPULATION /15% OF REGISTERED VOTERS

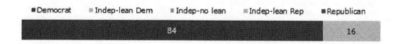

**Basic Description:** This largely blue-collar Democratic group is struggling financially and is generally cynical about government. Nearly half (47%) expect that they will not earn enough to lead the kind of life they want. Socially conservative and very religious.

**Defining values:** Critical of both business and government. View immigrants as an economic burden and a cultural threat. Supportive of environmental protection in general but concerned about the economic impact of environmental laws and regulations.

| KEY BELIEFS | General Public | Hard-Pressed Democrats |
|---|---|---|
| | % | % |
| Government is almost always wasteful and inefficient | 55 | 68 |
| Most corporations make a fair and reasonable profit | 39 | 16 |
| The government should do more to help needy Americans, even if it means going deeper into debt | 41 | 60 |
| Our country needs to continue making changes to give blacks equal rights with whites | 45 | 62 |
| Immigrants today are a burden on our country because they take our jobs, housing and health care | 44 | 76 |
| I often don't have enough money to make ends meet | 43 | 68 |
| It is necessary to believe in God in order to be moral and have good values | 48 | 75 |
| This country can't solve many of its important problems | 37 | 48 |

PEW RESEARCH CENTER 2011 Political Typology.

**Who they are:** A sizable number are non-Hispanic African American (35%), while 53% are non-Hispanic white. About seven in ten live in the South (48%) or Midwest (23%). Most (61%) are female. Two-thirds (68%) have only a high school education or less.

**Lifestyle notes:** Only 28% have a US passport. More than four in ten (43%) describe their household as "struggling." About one in five (21%) are out of work and seeking a job. 23% follow NASCAR. 61% regularly watch network evening news and 44% watch CNN.

# Solid Liberals

## 14% OF ADULT POPULATION /16% OF REGISTERED VOTERS

| ■ Democrat | ■ Indep-lean Dem | ■ Indep-no lean | ■ Indep-lean Rep | ■ Republican |

| 75 | 20 | 4 |

**Basic Description:** Politically engaged, Solid Liberals are strongly pro-government and hold liberal positions across the full range of political issues. They are one of the most secular groups. Two-thirds (67%) say they disagree with the Tea Party.

**Defining values:** Very supportive of regulation, environmental protection, and government assistance to the poor. Socially tolerant, supportive of the growing racial and ethnic diversity of the country. A majority (59%) say that religion is not that important to them.

| KEY BELIEFS | General Public | Solid Liberals |
|---|---|---|
| | % | % |
| Government often does a better job than people give it credit for | 39 | 74 |
| The government should do more to help needy Americans, even if it means going deeper into debt | 41 | 74 |
| Government regulation of business is necessary to protect the public interest | 47 | 86 |
| Most corporations make a fair and reasonable profit | 39 | 17 |
| Our country needs to continue making changes to give blacks equal rights with whites | 45 | 77 |
| Good diplomacy is the best way to ensure peace | 58 | 89 |
| The growing number of newcomers from other countries strengthens American society | 52 | 84 |
| Homosexuality should be accepted by society | 58 | 92 |
| PEW RESEARCH CENTER 2011 Political Typology. | | |

**Who they are:** Compared with the general public, more live in the Northeast (25%) and the West (28%). About half (49%) are college graduates , including 27% with postgraduate experience, the most of any group. 57% are female.

**Lifestyle notes:** Less likely than any other group to watch Fox News. About a third (34%) regularly listen to NPR, 21% regularly watch *The Daily Show,* 18% regularly read *The New York Times.* Six in ten (60%) use social networking sites. 59% have a US passport; 21% are first- or second-generation Americans. Many (42%) regularly buy organic foods.

# Bystanders

10% OF ADULT POPULATION /0% OF REGISTERED VOTERS

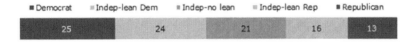

| ■ Democrat | ▨ Indep-lean Dem | ▪ Indep-no lean | ▨ Indep-lean Rep | ■ Republican |
|---|---|---|---|---|
| 25 | 24 | 21 | 16 | 13 |

**Basic Description:** Defined by their disengagement from the political process, either by choice or because they are ineligible to vote. They are highly unlikely to vote (61% say they seldom vote, and 39% volunteer that they never vote; none are registered to vote). Most follow government and public affairs only now and then (42%) or hardly at all (23%).

**Who they are:** Bystanders are overwhelmingly young (51% are under 30) and nearly half are Latino (38%) or black (9%). A third (33%) are first- or second-generation Americans. They are diverse in their political views though they lean Democratic, and their values more often align with the Democratic than the Republican groups. They also have much more favorable attitudes about the Democratic Party and its political figures than about the Republican Party. More than half (54%) have incomes under

$30,000 annually. Nearly two-thirds (64%) report that they or someone in their household were unemployed in the past year; 72% have only a high school education or less.

**Lifestyle notes:** Only 24% regularly read a daily newspaper. About a third (35%) regularly watch network evening news. Only 33% own their home, while 36% are looking for work or would prefer a full-time job to a part-time job they currently hold. Compared with most other groups, relatively few (25%) have a gun in the household, trade stocks in the market (8%), or have a labor union member in the household (5%).

Take the quiz: http://people-press.org/typology/quiz/?src=typology-report

# Chapter 9:
## It's a Matter of Faith and Politics

*The time has come that Christians must vote for honest men and take consistent ground in politics or the Lord will curse them ... Christians have been exceedingly guilty in this matter. But the time has come when they must act differently ... Christians seem to act as if they thought God did not see what they do in politics. But I tell you He does see it—and He will bless or curse this nation according to the course they [Christians] take [in politics].*
—Rev. Charles Finney, American revivalist

*Render therefore to Caesar the things that are Caesar's and to God the things that are God's.*
—Jesus the Christ, Luke 20:25

As a seminarian and church leader, I've been asked on occasion, "Does God belong in politics?" The answer is a resounding yes. "A person's religious beliefs inform who they are, the way they think, the truth they accept, and the very basis of their arguments," writes columnist Ken Connor. "To seek to remove religious speech from the public square is to establish secularism as the only acceptable mode of political discourse."[1]

The United States is fighting a civil war theologically speaking as evidenced by President Obama's claim that, "Whatever we once were, we're no longer a Christian nation. At least not just. We are also a Jewish nation, a Muslim nation, and a Buddhist nation, and a Hindu nation, and a nation of nonbelievers."[2] Whether the country is home to other faiths that are viable and deserving of respect is not the question. The question remains, is the United States a Christian nation? (It is curious that this is even debatable. Notice, the question is *not* whether the United States is a Muslim nation, or a Hindu nation, or a Buddhist nation. The answer is too obviously no, and no one would pose that question.)

Notwithstanding Obama's belief, the majority of Americans (85 percent are Christians) believe the Founding Fathers based America's founding documents on Judeo-Christian values. That the majority of these men were Christian is not challenged. Notwithstanding that the overwhelming majority of Americans are Christian and therefore the United States can clearly be considered a Christian nation, a debate continues over whether the nation was founded on Christian values. There are arguments on both sides. However, I believe that the basis for the Revolutionary War against Britain (fought by people who had fled religious persecution by the sovereign and saw themselves as God's elect), the history of the founding of the colonies, and the content of their state constitutions all support the idea that the US, if not a Christian nation, was certainly a nation built on Christian principles. Some prominent voices say likewise:

Former US Supreme Court Justice David J. Brewer said, "I have said enough to show that Christianity came to this country with the first colonists; has been powerfully identified with its rapid development, colonial and national, and today exists as a mighty factor in the life of the republic. This is a Christian nation ... [T]he calling of this republic a Christian nation is not a mere pretense but a recognition of an historical, legal and social truth."[3]

He continued, "Americans have always been extremely religious and overwhelmingly Christian. The 17th-century settlers founded their communities in America in large part for religious reasons. Eighteenth-century Americans saw their Revolution in religious and largely biblical terms. The Revolution reflected their 'covenant with God' and was a war between 'God's elect' and the British 'Antichrist.'"

Samuel Huntington writing an op-ed in The Wall Street Journal said, "Americans tend to have a certain catholicity toward religion: All deserve respect. Given this general tolerance of religious diversity, non-Christian faiths have little alternative but to recognize and accept America as a Christian society."[4]

There are also arguments against this proposition.

Alan Dershowitz writing an op-ed for The Huffington Post said, "Recently John McCain ... declared that "the Constitution established the United States of America as a Christian nation." What an ignoramus! McCain should go back to school and take Civics 1, where he might learn that the United States Constitution was called "the godless constitution"' by its opponents, because it was the first constitution in history not to include references to God or some dominant religion. The Constitution mentions religion only once, in prohibiting any religious test for holding office under the United States.

The Bill of Rights mentions religion twice, once in prohibiting an establishment of religion (a clear reference to any branch of Protestant Christianity, which was then the dominant religion) and a second time, in guaranteeing the free exercise of all religions. Several years after the ratification, the Senate ratified a treaty with the Barbary regime of Tripoli which expressly proclaimed that "the Government of the United States is not in any sense founded on the Christian religion."[5]

The argument against the belief that the US was built on Judeo-Christian values is steeped in fear of a God-centered culture and is made primarily by those who find no Creator in their own experience. That America was in fact built upon these values is the very reason it is loving, respectful, and tolerant toward all faiths. The Christian ethic requires this. Identify any Muslim country and then count its churches and temples. No Muslim countries allow them. This country is great because of God and the values it tries to uphold because of Him.

For non-Christians, the answer to the question may not be so easy. However, the majority of Americans believe the US is a Christian nation. This widely held belief makes America more Christian than Muslim, Buddhist, or otherwise despite Obama's declaration. This country is indeed fighting a civil war over religion; the proponents of a secular or irreligious philosophy (atheists and agnostics) are advancing an agenda undermining the values that make this nation great.

Hanging their hats on the Establishment Clause, which states that the government shall make no law establishing religion, the irreligious have taken prayer from our schools, the Ten Commandments from the steps of courthouses, and God out of the Pledge of Allegiance (from time to time). They have attempted to make same-sex marriage the new norm. These proponents even fight to take "In God We Trust" off of US currency. This secular movement has gained ground under the Obama administration.

Ken Connor writing for Townhall.com said, "The effort of America's Founders to prevent the establishment of a state religion has been twisted and reinterpreted to create an increasingly large gulf between religion and public life."[6] Our president contributed to this gulf when in April 2009 he asked Georgetown University to remove all religious signs and symbols from its hall before he delivered a speech there. Unfortunately, the university was only too willing to strip the hall of such symbols as banners bearing the letters *IHS,* an early Christian monogram of Jesus Christ's name. Obama's message was clear: religion has no place in the public square.

What must be understood about the Establishment Clause is the foresight the drafters had in protecting freedom for all faiths as promised in the First Amendment to the Constitution. They did this in response to religious oppression in England. America's government, unlike Great Britain's crown, would not impose a particular faith on its people and would not infringe upon the practice of one's faith. In the 1500s, the church in Great Britain became the Church of England, and the head of the church was also the head of state. This arrangement persists even today in England although the church has undergone much reform. This is not what the founders wanted for this nation, and they succeeded in preventing it.

# Call for Tolerance

For Christians, the mandate is clear. We are to operate *in* this world but not be *of* this world. To fulfill the Great Commission, we are supposed to be beacons of light to the world and spread the gospel of Jesus Christ, creating disciples. Jesus tells us, "Whoever acknowledges me before men, I will also acknowledge him before my Father in heaven. But whoever disowns me before men, I will disown him before my Father in heaven."[7]

Given Christ's words, it is difficult for Christians to divorce faith from our public discourse. If you are a follower of Christ, how will others know it unless you profess your faith publicly by word and deed? Granted, how, when, and where to do that are always up for debate, but whether to do so should not be.

Obama's directive to Georgetown University was an example of extreme multiculturalism. The effort to stifle the Christian faith—in this case, even the symbolism— is intolerable. Even the symbols of Christianity are too much for the multiculturalism crowd. They argue for tolerance—just not for the Christian faith. The trend to avoid giving offense in the name of a misplaced tolerance has gone too far. Instead of showing tolerance, those promoting it often offend others unnecessarily. Tolerance must be exercised in context.

My wife and I recently attended the annual banquet for an historic black charity. We sat at a table with a few friends but also some people we did not know. We happened to be next to a very nice Jewish couple.

The banquet began with an invocation by a prominent black pastor. He recited an eloquent opening prayer that omitted the typical Christian ending "In Jesus's name." At the end of the prayer, I leaned over to my wife and thought I had discreetly mentioned the glaring omission. I often take note of Christians who pray and leave out the name of Jesus to be sensitive to other faiths, because I've been asked to pray in a nonsectarian way in the homes of Jewish friends. The sweet Jewish couple overheard my comments. The husband disagreed and told me how very much they appreciated the pastor's tolerance. Here is how I responded to him:

When I hear a black pastor pray, I expect his faith to be evident. However, when I attend temple, a Seder, a bar mitzvah, bris, or other Jewish event—and I've attended many—I don't expect the rabbi to mention Christ to make me comfortable. When you attend a predominantly black event, it's a fair assumption it's a Christian crowd and you should therefore expect to hear the name of Jesus Christ in a prayer. That's what tolerance looks like, I said. He was silent.

I learned a lesson about tolerance in my own experience. Why should I expect my Jewish friends to welcome my Christ-centered prayer in their home? And why was I not sensitive enough to decline the invitation to pray over the meal or to pray and respect the tradition of their home? Tolerance cuts both ways.

Still, Christians have become the footstools of the irreligious. Afraid to own the Creator, we often bend to the cry for tolerance and hide in the shadows of an overbearing secular culture set against us. We are losing the battle; who will stand up for Christ in public without shame?

# The Christian and Poverty

When I have conversations with friends about being a conservative and Republican, they often agree with the values I hold. However, their biggest challenge with identifying with those labels is the perception that Republicans are for wealthy whites and big business only. No surprise.

In essence they say Republicans don't care about the poor and lack compassion for poor Americans. Many say Republicans have no moral or biblical compass because they believe the party doesn't care about the *least of these*. "Where are you feeding the hungry and clothing the naked?" they ask.

Often times they say, "Republicans preach that the people must pull themselves up by their own bootstraps." Then they follow that up with, "The only problem with that philosophy is that the people don't have any boots." It is this vantage point that leads most of my friends to the Democratic Party because they believe government is the only way to provide the boots.

It is clear that serving the poor is a virtue and a biblical mandate as discussed above in relation to social justice. There is no argument there. The question is who should serve them and how. The fundamental difference in our positions is that my liberal friends rely on government; I rely on the individual.

First, I don't believe the federal government is in the best position to know how best to serve the poor in my community. Government efforts to tax me so they can fund existing social programs that are broken are not the best use of my money. I am in a better position to know the needs of the poor in my community and to be charitable to them, to help the poor directly, and to see the fruit of my giving which perpetuates my philanthropy.

It's interesting to note that while liberals push for greater government spending on social programs fueled by tax dollars, conservatives give 30 percent more to charity than households headed by liberals.[8] It is also true that a large percentage of the conservative charitable giving is to religious institutions.

Second, I do believe there is a role that government can play in helping the needy across our nation. But that role is limited. The government's role must be focused on development, education, job skills training and the like and not on long-term welfare assistance. Financial assistance has to be short-term. This was accomplished in part under the welfare reform law in 1996 called the Personal Responsibility and Work Opportunity Reconciliation Act. Unfortunately by a policy directive in July 2012, President Obama removed the federal work requirement under the welfare reform law, the cornerstone of the legislation. Now, the current system will be sure to cripple the poor and keep them where they are – dependent on government.

Third, decades of government aid to the poor have failed. The war on poverty under President Lyndon Johnson began in 1964 when Congress signed the Economic Opportunity Act as part of the Great Society. At the time, poverty accounted for 19% of the population. Since then, federal and local governments have spent $15 trillion on the poverty campaign. Today, we spend $1 trillion dollars a year while the poor are 15.1 percent of the population and climbing rapidly.[9] Government has clearly failed to eradicate poverty yet we continue to poor money down the same failing system. How many more years or decades must we continue with this grand experiment? Throwing money at the poor doesn't change their circumstance; economic growth does.

Finally, individuals are best situated to help the poor starting with those in their own families. There are many examples in the Bible that reference helping the poor. They all revolve around individuals and communities. I have yet to see a reference in the Bible that supports or infers that the government should take money from the people to help the poor.

At the end of the day, the answer to the question – Where are you feeding the hungry and clothing the naked?- is clear. Conservatives are giving at levels that far exceed their liberal counterparts in their own backyards across the country but eradicating poverty is another matter. We have to break the current mindless government spending and create economic growth to put people to work and then to help them make better decisions for their future.

# The Christian and Politics

Don't let the title of this book fool you. This book is not a call for Christians or blacks to become Republicans. No, I am simply arguing that you must know the issues; you must line up the word of God with the issues, and vote on that basis. As a believer, you must know what God has to say about civil government and your role in the process.

First, God instituted government through Noah when He set every beast of the earth, every bird of the air, and every fish of the sea under the dominion of Noah and his sons.[10] God is interested in civil order. Further, He says, "Let every soul be subject to the governing authorities. For there is no authority except from God, and the authorities that exist are appointed by God."[11]

Moreover, the Bible tells us that we must honor those in government. We are told in 1 Peter 13–16, "Therefore, submit yourselves to every ordinance of man for the Lord's sake, whether to the king as supreme, or to governors, as to those who are sent by him for the punishment of evildoers and for the praise of those who do good. For this is the will of God, that by doing good you may put to silence the ignorance of foolish men."

It goes on to say, "Honor all people. Love the Brotherhood. Fear God. Honor the king." Honor is the operative word here.

The word *honor* means to revere or to bestow a distinction upon; to treat with respect. That is good. "Honor all people ... honor the king" (meaning Nero in this text). So we know that Christians are called to honor those in government and the ordinances or laws imposed upon us. The Christian code therefore acknowledges rules and authority. We are a law-abiding people. Government is God-ordained and not a secular institution.

Second, God gives the qualifications for civic leadership. Jethro, Moses's father-in-law, sees Moses driving himself crazy by managing all the tribes of Israel in the wilderness. He suggests that Moses "select from all the people able men, such as fear God, men of truth, hating covetousness; and place such over them to be rulers of thousands, rulers of hundreds, rulers of fifties, and rulers of ten."[12] Imagine electing our politicians today based on God's standard. Yes, as Christians, we should be concerned to elect officials who are able, fear God, and are people of truth.

Third, Christians must play an active role in influencing the policymakers who affect our communities. This is called politics.

Government can be responsible for oppressing the poor, allowing abortion, regulating exploitation of women and children in the sex trade, and deciding whether we live as free or oppressed people. How then can we not bring our faith to bear on politics to influence the very matters we must care about?

At the very least, we must do six simple things:

1. **Line up the word of God with the issues and vote based on biblical principles.**

2. **Pray daily for our nation's leaders.**

3. **Register to vote. (Which party you affiliate with is not the point.)**

4. **Be aware of whether the politicians you vote for support your values and biblical principles. This will require you to pay attention and do a little research if necessary.**

5. **Actively support godly men and women who stand for public office**

6. **Vote in every local and federal election**

It is a matter of faith to influence the policymakers in our communities. It's a matter of faith and politics.

# Epilogue

On Election Day, 2008, and during the events leading up to the ceremonial passing of the baton between George W. Bush and Barack Obama, I could not have been more proud for the United States to have elected a black man as president. There were multiple reasons why I did not vote for President Obama but chief among them was the certainty that with no experience operating a city, state, or business, his presidency would be a disaster. I didn't want that for the first black president.

Now, I publish this book virtually on the eve of the 2012 presidential election and I am looking back at four years of the effects of President Obama's policies. Because the president spent the first two years of his presidency on health care, he ignored the recession and the urgent need for job creation. Now we have a global economic crisis; we are now in a period of stagnant economic growth in the United States with unemployment above 8 percent for 43 consecutive months accounting for approximately 25 million unemployed; 1 in 6 people are now living in poverty with a record number of 47 million Americans on food stamps an increase of 65 percent since President Obama took office. During his four years in the Oval Office, President Obama accumulated $6 trillion in new debt which many claim to be more than the accumulated debt of the first 43 presidents before him. The country now has $16 trillion in national debt which many believe is unsustainable even for a super power such as the US. The European Union is collapsing with Greece leading the way. As if a global economic crisis isn't enough, the uncertainty of the president's foreign policy now has the Middle East on fire with attacks against our embassies in Libya (which included the murder of the US ambassador), Yemen, and Egypt, and with protests spreading like wild fires in the regions including Syria and Afghanistan; now wars are imminent between Iran and Israel as well as between China and Japan.

To an untrained eye, it seems the president simply doesn't have enough tools in the tool chest to handle these domestic and foreign challenges competently.

But for the resilience of the US in times past, it would be a time to run for the hills. But America is great and its people are greater.

The greatest challenge we face is not the dire economic and foreign relations crisis we find ourselves in. The greatest challenge we face is leadership. We sadly have a lack of leadership not only in the White House under the current president, but also in the Congress. American politics has not seen such polarized leadership in decades. This is what contributes to an America in crisis.

And black America is in crisis too. The plight of black America has not improved even after trillions of dollars have been spent on sustaining the safety net. Yes, many are eating and that's good. Yes, many are getting medical care through Medicaid and Medicare and that's good although often such care is inadequate. Veterans are being cared for and yes that's great. But people are still just getting by and blacks make up a fair number of those in the safety net of "I'm just getting by." Is this what the American dream has become? We brag about our safety net instead of delivering people from entitlement to prosperity?

While politicians blatantly lie to further their own political livelihood and while the country goes to hell in a hand basket, no one is in earnest leading blacks from entitlement to prosperity. Democrats accept the low and broken conditions of the black community by virtue of the fact that they represent these communities and see the brokenness daily and do very little. Republicans ignore the low and broken conditions of the black community since these communities are not Republican districts– for them, out of sight out of mind. The result: no one is dating the black voter.

Black unemployment was 15.8 percent at the end of 2011 which is double the national average. At the end of that year, black teenage unemployment was as high as 42.3 percent. Blacks likewise are declining in home ownership as home sales remain down and foreclosures have not yet abated. Blacks are disproportionately languishing during this Great Recession but they remain among the biggest consumers with a buying power of nearly $1 trillion annually. If blacks were a country, they'd be the 16th largest country in the world. Blacks are not leveraging their consumer power; instead they keep everyone else in business by their spending habits.

In order for the black community to survive, it has to first realize the political disenfranchisement it faces. The black community has been ignored by the first black president; it cannot get any worse in terms of political alienation. Entitlements have grown; a path to prosperity has not yet been paved. The tragedy is that some believe receiving more food stamps is a gift from the president. But free stuff eventually runs out.

My prayer is for each person, and particularly blacks, to understand their individual power as a citizen of this great country and not be taken for granted by any candidate or elected official who should be required to earn every vote. That's right, the politician works for the voter and they must earn every vote.

It is foolish to think that all blacks think and vote a certain way. Blacks are not monolithic; they simply have not yet brought themselves to marry their beliefs with their vote; when they do, the true diversity of the community will be evident.

However, we've been bamboozled to believe we cannot vote for a Republican because it is a racist party. That always puzzles me. Even if it was so, and it's not, I don't quite understand how blacks side with a party whose liberal ideology is counter to what most blacks believe. For instance, with the president's knowledge and before the Democratic National Convention began, the word God was stripped from the Democratic Party platform along with a reference to Jerusalem as the capital of Israel; when conservative media began reporting on the platform's glaring omissions, the Democrats moved swiftly to re-insert God into the platform. When the party chair later made a motion during the convention to re-insert the reference to God and Jerusalem, the Democratic delegates booed and booed loudly not once, not twice, but three times in protest to the inclusion of God in the platform! Blacks are overwhelmingly people of faith but yet they have no problem standing shoulder-to-shoulder with a fair number of Godless delegates.

Another example: The president, a liberal Democrat, supports same-sex marriage. Blacks overwhelmingly across the country are opposed to same-sex marriage yet with few exceptions they stand in support of a party who does not share that value.

Another example: The president, a liberal Democrat, failed to protect an infant born alive after a partial birth abortion in Illinois. Correct. He is not only a supporter of abortion but he is a supporter of partial birth abortion. As president, he has the chance to appoint Supreme Court justices who would support his worldview. This extreme abortion position is as far left as it can get and is not widely shared by the black community yet they stood in line and will stand in line again to vote for him.

At what point will the conservative values that older blacks share begin to matter in elections? The current generation of blacks has lost most of the conservative values held by their parents and thus the theme of this book for them to return to the traditional values of our recent past; if we fail to instill them now, the "value vote" will likely never return and they will continue to support the policies of a party that does not truly regard them.

Why? Blacks vote for Democrats because they vote their emotions and not the issues which should be the most important factors in an election. The thought of challenging the racial ideas that have been indoctrinated into the black psyche by the liberal media and the liberals themselves is too much of an emotional hurdle given the racial injustices of the past. I understand that few people could pass up the opportunity to elect the first black president but enough already. This is not about emotion or color; it's about faith and politics.

While blacks seem to be satisfied with their current lot, the deck chairs are shifting all around them and they are not paying attention.

Democrats and Republicans have aggressively pursued the Latino vote during the 2012 presidential election. Flying in and out of Florida and Los Angeles courting the various Latino groups; the president even passed policies that discouraged deportation and even created circumstances by Executive Order where groups of Latinos could obtain work visas that amounted to a form of amnesty. I cannot tell you how many Jamaicans and Haitians are run out of the US for violating immigration laws while Mexicans specifically are coddled. Blacks are invisible to this administration. Recall, President Obama refused for the third consecutive year to even attend the NAACP annual banquet. Blacks are falling away from the table of political influence. For example, district lines in large cities like Los Angeles are being redrawn which is changing the face of local politics in Los Angeles; districts for Latino representatives are being expanded while the districts for many black representatives are shrinking. Eventually, blacks will also be currying favor from Latino representatives in order to be heard in the political arena because blacks will not be represented by members of their own community in local government.

When I am called on to promote my conservative Republican position, I am invariably asked what candidate Mitt Romney will do for the black community if he were elected president. I am always surprised by the question.

I quickly retort, before you ask what will Romney do for blacks, please first tell me what the first black president has done for blacks? There is no response.

Often in those same discussions, I am asked how I can be openly conservative and Republican. It's easy. I line up my faith with my vote. First, I am Pro-Life and I am against same-sex marriage just to name a few of the social issues that agree squarely with the Republican Party platform. Second, I am for a small limited government that keeps its hands out of my pocket, promotes personal responsibility, and applauds personal achievement. America is about prosperity achieved through hard work and not by redistributive schemes to take from the rich as President Obama likes to promote. Third, I am for the three founding principles of America which can be summarized as (1) "In God We Trust"- we are a nation built on Judeo-Christian values. We have a code of faith that drives goodness within us. (2) E pluribus unum (Out of many, one); Americans are proudly bound together like no other recent culture united as one nation, under God, indivisible with liberty and justice for all; and (3) Liberty. We are a free people. Free to succeed or free to fail and free to pursue our own happiness without fear of government intrusion.

Finally, I never understood why blacks would be content with not having a seat at the table when Republicans are in power. Blacks should be represented in all corridors of influence; politics is no exception. When Republicans regain the White House, I will be there looking for the benefits for my inner city community. Where will you be?

With God's help, let's reclaim our future, together!

-Marc T. Little

# *Notes*

## Introduction

1. Department of Commerce. "United States Census Bureau." census. gov. 2010. http://www.census.gov/ (accessed August 25, 2012).

2. Robert Balfanz, John M. Bridgeland, Mary Bruce, Joanna Hornig Fox. "Building a Grad Nation." America's Promise. 2012. www. americaspromise.org (accessed September 12, 2012).

3. The Annie E. Casey Foundation. "Kids Count." Data Center Kids Count. 2010. http://datacenter.kidscount.org/data/acrossstates/ Rankings.aspx?ind=107 (accessed August 25, 2012).

4. Center for Disease Control. "Abortion Survellance: United States 2008." Center for Disease Control and Prevention/MMWR. November 25, 2011. www.cdc.gov (accessed August 25, 2012).

5. The Pew Research Center, The Black and White of Pubic Opinion. October 31, 2005. http://www.people-press.org/2005/10/31/the-black-and-white-of-public-opinion/ (accessed August 25, 2012).

6. Ibid.

# Chapter 2.

# My Politics: What I Believe

1. FactCheck, "Obama and 'Infanticide'." Factcheck. August 25, 2008. http://www.factcheck.org/2008/08/obama-and-infanticide/ (accessed August 25, 2012).

2. Kost, K., Henshaw, S., Carlin, L. "US Teen Pregnancies, Births, and Abortions: National and State Trends and Trends by Race and Ethnicity." Guttmacher Institute. January 2010. http://www.guttmacher.org/pubs/USTPtrends.pdf (accessed August 25, 2012).

3. Center for Disease Control. "Abortion Surveillance: United States 2008." Center for Disease Control and Prevention/MMWR. November 25, 2011. www.cdc.gov (accessed August 25, 2012).

4. League, American Life. Racists and Eugenicists Statements by Margaret Sanger, The Founder of Planned Parenthood Founder. n.d. blackquillandink.com/wp-content/.../01/margaret-sanger-quotes.pdf (accessed August 25, 2012).

5. Foster, Daniel. "Jesse Jackson's Evolving Standard of Genocide." National Review Online. November 11, 2010. http://www.nationalreview.com/corner/253146/jesse-jacksons-evolving-standards-genocide-daniel-foster (accessed August 25, 2012).

6. Surdin, Karl Vick and Ashley. The Washington Post, November 7, 2008.

7. FactReal. May 8, 2010. http://factreal.wordpress.com/2010/05/08/mexico-vs-united-states-mexican-immigration-laws-are-tougher/ (accessed August 25, 2012).

8. FinAid. The Smart Student Guide to Financial Aid. 2012. http://www.finaid.org/otheraid/undocumented.phtml (accessed August 25, 2012).

9. Walker, Lee H. Rediscovering Black Conservatism. Chicago: The Heatland Institute, 2009, page 27, citing Booker T. Washington, Up From Slavery, 1901.

10. Mark R. Levin, Liberty and Tyranny, 2009, pg 62.

11. Censky, Annalyn. Black Unemployment: Highest in 27 Years. September 2, 2011. http://money.cnn.com/2011/09/02/news/economy/black_unemployment_rate/index.htm (accessed August 25, 2012).

## Chapter 3

## From Republican to Democrat: The Black Political Journey

1. Barton, David. Setting The Record Straight: American History in Black and White. Aledo: WallBuilder Press, 2004, pg.11

2. Ibid.

3. Ibid. 13.

4. Ibid. 11.

5. Ibid. 23.

6. Ibid. 24.

7. Ibid. 25.

8. Ibid.

9. Ibid. 30, quoting Confederate Vice President Alexander Stephens.

10. Ibid. 33.

11. Foner, Eric. History Matters. 1988. http://historymatters.gmu.edu/impeach2.html (accessed August 25, 2012).

12. Henry George School of Social Science. Land and Freedom. 2012. http://www.landandfreedom.org/ushistory/us15.htm (accessed August 25, 2012)

13. Lopez, Mark Hugo. Dissecting the 2008 Electorate. April 30, 2009. http://pewresearch.org/pubs/1209/racial-ethnic-voters-presidential-election (accessed August 25, 2012).

14. Barton, David. Setting The Record Straight: American History in Black and White. Aledo: WallBuilder Press, 2004, pg.45.

15. Fauntroy, Michael K. Republicans and the Black Vote. Boulder: Lynne Rienner, 2006, p 31.

16. Barton, David. Setting The Record Straight: American History in Black and White. Aledo: WallBuilder Press, 2004, pg.45.

17. Shogan, Jennifer E. Manning and Colleen J. "African American Members of the United States Congress:1870-2011." Congressional Research Service. April 8, 2011. www.crs.gov (accessed August 25, 2012).

18. Barton, David. Setting The Record Straight: American History in Black and White. Aledo: WallBuilder Press, 2004, pg.48

19. Ibid. 50.

20. Ibid. 81.

21. Ibid. 83.

22. Ibid. 84.

23. Ibid. 86.

24. Taylor, Quintard. "The Grandfather Clause: 1898-1915." BlackPast.org. 2011. http://www.blackpast.org/?q=aah/grandfather-clause-1898-1915 (accessed August 25, 2012).

25. Fauntroy, Michael K. Republicans and the Black Vote. Boulder: Lynne Rienner, 2006, pg. 42.

26. Ibid. 43.

27. Ibid. 44.

28. Ibid.

29. Barton, David. Setting The Record Straight: American History in Black and White. Aledo: WallBuilder Press, 2004, pg.120.

30. Ibid. 45.

31. Ibid.

32. Ibid. 46.

33. Ibid.

34. Ibid. 47.

35. Barton, David. Setting The Record Straight: American History in Black and White. Aledo: WallBuilder Press, 2004, pg.121.

36. Fauntroy, Michael K. Republicans and the Black Vote. Boulder: Lynne Rienner, 2006, pg. 48.

37. Contributors, Wikipedia. "Civil Rights Act of 1964." Wikipedia, Free Encyclopedia. August 23, 2012; http://en.wikipedia.org/w/

index.php?title=Civil_Rights_Act_of_1964&oldid=508853432
(accessed August 25, 2012).

38. Barton, David. Setting The Record Straight: American History in
Black and White. Aledo: WallBuilder Press, 2004, pg.131.

# Chapter 4

# The Train from Washington is One
# Hundred Years Overdue

1. Murray, Sara. "Nearly Half of U.S. Lives in Household Receiving
Government Benefit." The Wall Street Journal. October 5, 2011.
http://blogs.wsj.com/economics/2011/10/05/nearly-half-of-
households-receive-some-government-benefit/ (accessed August
25, 2012).

2. Fumento, Michael. "Is the Great Society to Blame? If Not, Why
Have Problems Worsened Since '60's?" Investor's Business Daily/
Michael Fumento. June 19, 1992. http://fumento.com/economy/
greatsociety.html (accessed August 25, 2012).

3. Vuk, Vendran. "The Welfare State's Attack on the Family." Mises
Daily. July 12, 2006. www.mises.org (accessed August 25, 2012).

4. Fumento, Michael. "Is the Great Society to Blame? If Not, Why
Have Problems Worsened Since '60's?" Investor's Business Daily/
Michael Fumento. June 19, 1992. http://fumento.com/economy/
greatsociety.html (accessed August 25, 2012).

5. Department of Commerce. "United States Census Bureau." census.
gov. 1997. http://www.census.gov/ (accessed August 25, 2012).

6.  Rector, Robert. "Reducing Poverty by Revitalizing Marriage in Low-Income Communties: A Memo to President-elect Obama." The Heritage Foundation. January 13, 2009. http://www.heritage.org/research/reports/2009/01/reducing-poverty-by-revitalizing-marriage-in-low-income-communities (accessed August 25, 2012).

7.  Department of Education. "Digest of Education Statistics: 2011." National Center for Education Statistics. 2012. http://nces.ed.gov/programs/digest/d11/ch_2.asp (accessed August 25, 2012); rate is 9.3 percent compared with 5.2 percent in 2009; the dropout rate for Hispanics 17.6 percent for the same period.

8.  Barton, David. Setting The Record Straight: American History in Black and White. Aledo: WallBuilder Press, 2004, pg.89.

# Chapter 5

# The Pied Pipers

1.  Entrepreneur Staff. "Steve Jobs: An Extraordinary Career." Entrepreneur Media. 2011. http://www.entrepreneur.com/article/197538# (accessed August 25, 2012).

2.  National Park Service. "We Shall Overcome." National Park Service, US Department of the Interior. n.d. http://www.nps.gov/nr/travel/civilrights/intro.htm (accessed August 25, 2012).

3.  Entreprenuer Staff. "Madam CJ Walker: From Poverty to Prosperity." Entrepreneur Media. October 10, 2008. http://www.entrepreneur.com/article/197708 (accessed August 25, 2012).

4.  CNN. "Senate Approves Iraq War Resolution." CNN. October 11, 2002. http://articles.cnn.com/2002-10-11/politics/

iraq.us_1_biological-weapons-weapons-inspectors-iraq?_
s=PM:ALLPOLITICS (accessed August 25, 2012).

5. Contributors, Wikipedia, "Nelson Mandela." Wikipedia, The Free
Encyclopedia. August 24, 2012. http://en.wikipedia.org/w/index.
php?title=Special:Cite&page=Nelson_Mandela&id=508939597
(accessed August 25, 2012).

# Chapter 6

# A Letter to the Family

1. Moynihan, Daniel Patrick. "The Negro Family: The Case for
National Action." US Department of Labor. March 1965. http://
www.dol.gov/oasam/programs/history/webid-meynihan.htm
(accessed August 25, 2012).

2. Ibid.

3. Contributors, Wikipedia, "The Negro Family: The Case For
National Action." Wikipedia, The Free Encyclopedia. April 17,
2012. http://en.wikipedia.org/wiki/The_Negro_Family:_The_
Case_For_National_Action (accessed August 27, 2012).

4. Department of Commerce. "United States Census Bureau." census.
gov. 2009. http://www.census.gov/ (accessed August 25, 2012).

5. Foster, Daniel. "Jesse Jackson's Evolving Standard of Genocide."
National Review Online. November 11, 2010. http://www.
nationalreview.com/corner/253146/jesse-jacksons-evolving-
standards-genocide-daniel-foster (accessed August 25, 2012).

6. The Holy Bible, New International Version®:Ac 12:7. Grand Rapids:
The Zondervan Corporation, © 1973, 1978, 1984.

7. Sodano, Cardinal Angelo. "Compendium of the Social Doctrine of the Church." Vatican. 2004. http://www.vatican.va/roman_curia/pontifical_councils/justpeace/documents/rc_pc_justpeace_doc_20060526_compendio-dott-soc_en.html (accessed August 25, 2012).

8. Contributors, Wikipedia, "Social Justice." Wikipedia, Free Encyclopedia. August 26, 2012. http://en.wikipedia.org/w/index.php?title=Social_justice&oldid=509175958 (accessed August 27, 2012).

9. O'Neill, Ben. "The Injustice of Social Justice." Ludwig von Mises Institute. March 16, 2011. http://mises.org/daily/5099/The-Injustice-of-Social-Justice (accessed August 25, 2012).

10. Horowitz, David. Eagle Forum. January 2009. http://www.eagleforum.org/psr/2009/jan09/psrjan09.html (accessed August 25, 2012).

11. Eagle Forum. "Social Justice: Code Word for Anti-Americanism." Eagle Forum. January 2009. http://www.eagleforum.org/psr/2009/jan09/psrjan09.html (accessed August 25, 2012).

12. The Holy Bible, New International Version." 2 Thess. 3:10–13 Grand Rapids: Zondervan Corporation, 1973, 1978, 1984.

13. The Holy Bible, New International Version." Prov. 22:6 Grand Rapids: Zondervan Corporation, 1973, 1978, 1984.

14. The Holy Bible, New International Version." 1 Cor. 13:4–8 Grand Rapids: Zondervan Corporation, 1973, 1978, 1984.

# Chapter 7

## A Challenge to the Republican Party

1. Emsellem, Maurice ans Michelle Natividad Rodriguez. "65 Million Need Not Apply." National Employment Law Project. March 10, 2011. http://www.nelp.org/site/issues/category/criminal_records_ and_employment/ (accessed August 27, 2012).

2. Levin, Mark R. Liberty and Tyranny. New York: Threshold Editions, 2009, pg 204

# Chapter 8

## Are You a Democrat or a Republican? Take the Test

1. The Pew Research Center. "Beyond Red and Blue: The Political Typology." The Pew Research Center. May 4, 2011. http://www. people-press.org/2011/05/04/beyond-red-vs-blue-the-political- typology/ (accessed August 25, 2012).

# Chapter 9

## It's a Matter of Faith and Politics

1. Ken Connor, "Obama Vetoes Religion in the Public Square," Townhall.com, April 26, 2009.

2. Ibid.

3. Brewer, David Josiah. The United States: A Christian Nation. Winston, 1905.

4. Huntington, Samuel P. "Under God'—Michael Newdow Is Right: Atheists Are Outsiders in America." Wall Street Journal, Op-Ed, June 16, 2004.

5. Dershowitz, Alan M. "McCain and the Godless Constitution." Huffington Post, Op-Ed, October 3, 2007.

6. Connor, Ken. Obama Vetoes Religion in the Public Square, Townhall.com, April 26, 2009. n.d. http://townhall.com/columnists/kenconnor/2009/04/26/obama_vetoes_religion_in_the_public_square (accessed August 25, 2012).

7. The Holy Bible, New International Version." Matt. 10:32–33 Grand Rapids: Zondervan Corporation, 1973, 1978, 1984.

8. Nicholas, Kristof. "Bleeding Heart Tightwads." New York Times, December 20, 2008, citing Brooks, Arthur, "Who Really Cares: The Surprising Truth About Compassionate Conservatism, Who Gives, Who Doesn't and Why it Matters,"(Basic Books) 2006.

9. Tanner, Michael D. "The American Welfare State: How We Spend Nearly $1 Trillion a Year Fighting Poverty--And Fail." cato.org. April 11, 2012. http://www.cato.org/publications/policy-analysis/american-welfare-state-how-we-spend-nearly-$1-trillion-year-fighting-poverty-fail. (accessed August 25, 2012).

10. The Holy Bible, New International Version." Gen. 9:17. Grand Rapids: Zondervan Corporation, 1973, 1978, 1984.

11. The Holy Bible, New International Version." Rom. 13:1. Grand Rapids: Zondervan Corporation, 1973, 1978, 1984.

12. The Holy Bible, New International Version." Ex. 18:21. Grand Rapids: Zondervan Corporation, 1973, 1978, 1984.

# Bibliography

Barton, David. Setting The Record Straight: American History in Black and White. Aledo: WallBuilder Press, 2004.

Brewer, David Josiah. The United States: A Christian Nation. Winston, 1905.

Censky, Annalyn. Black Unemployment: Highest in 27 Years. September 2, 2011. http://money.cnn.com/2011/09/02/news/economy/black_unemployment_rate/index.htm (accessed August 25, 2012).

Center for Disease Control. "Abortion Survellance: United States 2008." Center for Disease Control and Prevention/MMWR. November 25, 2011. www.cdc.gov (accessed August 25, 2012).

CNN. "Senate Approves Iraq War Resolution." CNN. October 11, 2002. http://articles.cnn.com/2002-10-11/politics/iraq.us_1_biological-weapons-weapons-inspectors-iraq?_s=PM:ALLPOLITICS (accessed August 25, 2012).

Connor, Ken. Obama Vetoes Religion in the Public Square, Townhall.com, April 26, 2009. n.d. http://townhall.com/columnists/kenconnor/2009/04/26/obama_vetoes_religion_in_the_public_square (accessed August 25, 2012).

Contributors, Wikipedia. "Civil Rights Act of 1964." Wikipedia, Free Encyclopedia. August 23, 2012. http://en.wikipedia.org/w/index.php?title=Civil_Rights_Act_of_1964&oldid=508853432 (accessed August 25, 2012).

—. "Nelson Mandela." Wikipedia, The Free Encyclopedia. August 24, 2012. http://en.wikipedia.org/w/index.php?title=Special:Cite&page=Nelson_Mandela&id=508939597 (accessed August 25, 2012).

—. "Social Justice." Wikipedia, Free Encyclopedia. August 26, 2012. http://en.wikipedia.org/w/index.php?title=Social_justice&oldid=509175958 (accessed August 27, 2012).

—. "The Negro Family: The Case For National Action." Wikipedia, The Free Encyclopedia. April 17, 2012. http://en.wikipedia.org/wiki/The_Negro_Family:_The_Case_For_National_Action (accessed August 27, 2012).

Department of Commerce. "United States Census Bureau." census.gov. 2010. http://www.census.gov/ (accessed August 25, 2012).

Department of Education. "Digest of Education Statistics: 2011." National Center for Education Statistics. 2012. http://nces.ed.gov/programs/digest/d11/ch_2.asp (accessed August 25, 2012).

Dershowitz, Alan M. "McCain and the Godless Constitution." Huffington Post, Op-Ed, October 3, 2007.

Eagle Forum. "Social Justice: Code Word for Anti-Americanism." Eagle Forum. January 2009. http://www.eagleforum.org/psr/2009/jan09/psrjan09.html (accessed August 25, 2012).

Emsellem, Maurice, Michelle Natividad Rodriguez. "65 Million Need Not Apply." National Employment Law Project. March 10, 2011. http://www.nelp.org/site/issues/category/criminal_records_and_employment/ (accessed August 27, 2012).

Entrepreneur Staff. "Steve Jobs: An Extraordinary Career." Entrepreneur Media. 2011. http://www.entrepreneur.com/article/197538# (accessed August 25, 2012).

Entreprenuer Staff. "Madam CJ Walker: From Poverty to Prosperity." Entrepreneur Media. October 10, 2008. http://www.entrepreneur.com/article/197708 (accessed August 25, 2012).

FactCheck. "Obama and 'Infanticide'." Factcheck. August 25, 2008. http://www.factcheck.org/2008/08/obama-and-infanticide/ (accessed August 25, 2012).

FactReal. May 8, 2010. http://factreal.wordpress.com/2010/05/08/mexico-vs-united-states-mexican-immigration-laws-are-tougher/ (accessed August 25, 2012).

Fauntroy, Michael K. Republicans and the Black Vote. Boulder: Lynne Rienner, 2006.

FinAid. The Smart Student Guide to Financial Aid. 2012. http://www.finaid.org/otheraid/undocumented.phtml (accessed August 25, 2012).

Foner, Eric. History Matters. 1988. http://historymatters.gmu. edu/impeach2.html (accessed August 25, 2012).

Foster, Daniel. "Jesse Jackson's Evolving Standard of Genocide." National Review Online. November 11, 2010. http://www. nationalreview.com/corner/253146/jesse-jacksons-evolving-standards-genocide-daniel-foster (accessed August 25, 2012).

Fumento, Michael. "Is the Great Society to Blame? If Not, Why Have Problems Worsened Since '60's?" Investor's Business Daily/ Michael Fumento. June 19, 1992. http://fumento.com/economy/ greatsociety.html (accessed August 25, 2012).

Henry George School of Social Science. Land and Freedom. 2012. http://www.landandfreedom.org/ushistory/us15.htm (accessed August 25, 2012).

Horowitz, David. Eagle Forum. January 2009. http://www. eagleforum.org/psr/2009/jan09/psrjan09.html (accessed August 25, 2012).

Huntington, Samuel P. "Under God'—Michael Newdow Is Right: Atheists Are Outsiders in America." Wall Street Journal, Op-Ed, June 16, 2004.

Kost, K., Henshaw, S., Carlin, L. "US Teen Pregnancies, Births, and Abortions: National and State Trends and Trends by Race and Ethnicity." Guttmacher Institute. January 2010. http:// www.guttmacher.org/pubs/USTPtrends.pdf (accessed August 25, 2012).

League, American Life. Racists and Eugenicists Statements by Margaret Sanger, The Founder of Planned Parenthood Founder. n.d. blackquillandink.com/wp-content/.../01/margaret-sanger-quotes.pdf (accessed August 25 25, 2012).

Levin, Mark R. Liberty and Tyranny. New York: Threshold Editions, 2009.

Lopez, Mark Hugo. Dissecting the 2008 Electorate. April 30, 2009. http://pewresearch.org/pubs/1209/racial-ethnic-voters-presidential-election (accessed August 25, 2012).

Moynihan, Daniel Patrick. "The Negro Family: The Case for National Action." US Department of Labor. March 1965. http://www.dol.gov/oasam/programs/history/webid-meynihan.htm (accessed August 25, 2012).

Murray, Sara. "Nearly Half of U.S. Lives in Household Receiving Government Benefit." The Wall Street Journal. October 5, 2011. http://blogs.wsj.com/economics/2011/10/05/nearly-half-of-households-receive-some-government-benefit/ (accessed August 25, 2012).

National Park Service. "We Shall Overcome." National Park Service, US Department of the Interior. n.d. http://www.nps.gov/nr/travel/civilrights/intro.htm (accessed August 25, 2012).

Nicholas, Kristof. "Bleeding Heart Tightwads." New York Times, December 20, 2008.

O'Neill, Ben. "The Injustice of Social Justice." Ludwig von Mises Institute. March 16, 2011. http://mises.org/daily/5099/The-Injustice-of-Social-Justice (accessed August 25, 2012).

Rector, Robert. "Reducing Poverty by Revitalizing Marriage in Low-Income Communties: A Memo to President-elect Obama." The Heritage Foundation. January 13, 2009. http://www.heritage.org/research/reports/2009/01/reducing-poverty-by-revitalizing-marriage-in-low-income-communities (accessed August 25, 2012).

Rev. Clenard Childress, Jr. Blackgenocide.org. 2012. http://blackgenocide.org/black.html (accessed August 25, 2012).

Robert Balfanz, John M. Bridgeland, Mary Bruce, Joanna Hornig Fox. "Building a Grad Nation." America's Promise. 2012. www.americaspromise.org (accessed September 12, 2012).

Shogan, Jennifer E. Manning and Colleen J. "African American Members of the United States Congress:1870-2011." Congressional Research Service. April 8, 2011. www.crs.gov (accessed August 25, 2012).

Sodano, Cardinal Angelo. "Compendium of the Social Doctrine of the Church." Vatican. 2004. http://www.vatican.va/roman_curia/pontifical_councils/justpeace/documents/rc_pc_justpeace_doc_20060526_compendio-dott-soc_en.html (accessed August 25, 2012).

Surdin, Karl Vick and Ashley. The Washington Post, November 7, 2008.

Tanner, Michael D. "The American Welfare State: How We Spend Nearly $1 Trillion a Year Fighting Poverty--And Fail." cato.org. April 11, 2012. http://www.cato.org/publications/policy-analysis/american-welfare-state-how-we-spend-nearly-$1-trillion-year-fighting-poverty-fail. (accessed August 25, 2012).

Taylor, Quintard. "The Grandfather Clause: 1898-1915." BlackPast. org. 2011. http://www.blackpast.org/?q=aah/grandfather-clause-1898-1915 (accessed August 25, 2012).

The Annie E. Casey Foundation. "Kids Count." Data Center Kids Count. 2010. http://datacenter.kidscount.org/data/acrossstates/Rankings.aspx?ind=107 (accessed August 25, 2012).

"The Holy Bible, New International Version." Ac 12:7. Grand Rapids: Zondervan Corporation, 1973, 1978, 1984.

The Pew Research Center. "Beyond Red and Blue: The Political Typology." The Pew Research Center. May 4, 2011. http://www.people-press.org/2011/05/04/beyond-red-vs-blue-the-political-typology/ (accessed August 25, 2012).

—. The Black and White of Pubic Opinion. October 31, 2005. http://www.people-press.org/2005/10/31/the-black-and-white-of-public-opinion/ (accessed August 25, 2012).

Vuk, Vendran. "The Welfare State's Attack on the Family." Mises Daily. July 12, 2006. www.mises.org (accessed August 25, 2012).

Walker, Lee H. Rediscovering Black Conservatism. Chicago: The Heatland Institute, 2009.

Made in the USA
Middletown, DE
10 August 2021